the unco project

Essays from the edge of seventeen: A teenager's worldview

Shraddha Anu Shekar

INDIA • SINGAPORE • MALAYSIA

ISBN 979-8-89233-585-0

DEDICATION

To my Kittaa Thaathaa,

- Thank you for engaging with me in some of the best discussions I've had.

To my friends:

- You help me fulfill the constant urge to discuss anything and everything under the sun. Be it light-hearted banter or introspective, philosophical questions, I learn more each time. I look forward to learning more from you!

To my mentors:

- I would like to thank my teachers, guides, and non-teaching staff from The School, KFI.
- Thank you for providing an environment that is both physically and emotionally comfortable. The space to sit and ponder, and the space to explore questions helped create this book. Thank you for further nurturing my love for writing and instilling a new passion for research work!

Shraddha Anu Shekar
the unco explorer

Contents

What's the Unco Project?

In "The Unco Project", my essays explore aspects under three overarching headings:

Politics and History

Analysis and review of popular media, and

The environment.

The media I view around me, be they books, essays, movies/films, advertisements, songs and the like - have brought up some important questions for me with regards to everyday life.

I have written five books since I was nine years old. '***The Unco Project***', my sixth book, is the first book delving majorly into the world of non-fiction writing.

But why unco?

Unco is actually a word in itself - something I discovered quite recently too!! Unco means something that is unusual or remarkable.

As 'The Unco Explorer', I aim to explore topics and phenomena that particularly stand out to me.

My interest in the broad world of Humanities and English propelled me to take up History, Sociology, Environmental Science and Economics as my main subjects in high school (11th and 12th grade).

Both the fiction and non-fiction aspects of the book reflect my current personal views that are subject to change. My ideals and opinions are evolving. This book is meant additionally to be a record of the values I hold at present.

Disclaimer: The book is a collection of my opinions, and is not meant to be offensive to any particular group or community of people.

POLITICS AND HISTORY

CHAPTER ONE

AS THE SUN ROSE: A Sri Lankan Youth's Yearning

A fresh recruit was ready to prove himself. Yohan was 21 years old and was in the Sri Lankan Army when the war started. One day, he was hailed as the youngest of the forces. The next, he was crouched behind a mound, trying not to be shot.

No one had expected the militants to be capable of carrying out the promises they had catered to the Tamils and believers of the Tamil Eelam.

They all believed - according to Yohan, deluded themselves - into thinking that the rift had subsided and that things could only get better.

Now a 28-year-old amputee who had long since left the armed forces, Yohan still carried the baggage of war with him. It haunted him, not allowing him to blink.

Memories flashed in front of him, much like the bullets that had changed the trajectory of his dreams on that fateful day seven years ago. The Internet's rendition of events did not quite encapsulate the void in him.

A freighter for Indonesia was to leave from Trincomalee around 4 in the morning. It would be the only way Yohan could leave Sri Lanka for good. He worried about all the things that could go wrong. The most challenging part was not knowing whether he could escape the nightmarish landscape when he fell asleep - *if* he fell asleep.

He decided to visit the Old Fort one last time - a keepsake for him to reminisce about whenever he would inevitably miss his home.

As the evening drawled into night time, Yohan slowly started making his way from his shack to the Old Fort. He used his usual route through the tapering road. The already incommodious path was covered in posters of the various political factions, each hoping to capitalize off the people's suffering. It was definitely a depressing sight to be reminded of wherever he went. The Old Fort was his haven, where he could pretend he lived a normal life. As the days passed, it felt like Yohan leaned in more and more with that delusional community he often grumbled about.

Upon entering the premises through the "secret" entrance behind the Old Fort, Yohan lay down on the less-than-pristine lawn, long overgrown with weeds. He remembered the days he would escape to this very Fort as a child. Hiding among the rubble while playing hide and seek with friends he had just made, and sitting in a time-out corner all sulky after being caught—the days when worries had no place.

Impulsiveness was not a tendency Yohan frequented in his actions, but something in him prompted him to explore that space once more. His muscle memory did not fail him as he walked the same path, he had done for most of his childhood. He was surprised to see the place unchanged, just as he recalled. Except something *had* changed. The debris seemed a little too clean as if someone had taken the painstaking effort of rearranging it to resemble the arrangement of the remnants from the past.

As he cleared the rubbish, he saw something unexpected underneath: a glint of metal, almost like a pipe, hidden away. Yohan's shortness of breath did nothing to deter him from determining what exactly was below this mystery. And there stood a pig in a cage, an exact depiction of the image Yohan had in his mind when he read Animal Farm for the first time. Its eyes seemed to cry out to him, which tugged at his heartstrings to do something, anything to give it momentary respite.

He gave up on the idea of forcing the cage open pretty quickly but found a latch with a lock on the side. Picking up some heavier rock pieces, he smashed the lock open. The pig seemed to have lost most of its leg strength. Yohan took it upon himself to carry the pig out and show it the daylight and space it had been craving for however long it had been trapped there.

As he set the pig down on the somewhat grassy terrain, his flip phone pinged with a notification.

It was one of the few luxuries he allowed himself to possess. Yohan read out the message - it was from his acquaintance in Indonesia. The message was a reminder to somehow get on the freighter and reach Sumatra Island safely; the state of his arrival would decide the course of action on land.

He wondered what to do with the pig. "I don't think neither you *nor* the butcher would like each other…" he muttered to the creature that looked at him with stars in its eyes.

He quickly realised that he did not have it in him to leave the pig; free from its cage yet abandoned once again. Yohan went back to the area where he found the pig and found some twine inside its cage. "I guess you have no choice but to come along with me then."

He wound the twine carefully around the pig's neck to create a leash. Once the pig seemed satisfied navigating its new surroundings, Yohan led it outside the Old Fort. The two walked for what seemed like hours until they reached the port. Yohan swiftly recognized the cargo ship they were to board and picked up the pig like it weighed nothing. Sneaking past the one dozy guard, the two boarded the ship. Holding the pig as close as he could, Yohan stalked most of the ship before ducking under some tarpaulined crates. He could see the feet of a group - maybe a family - sticking out of the tarpaulin a couple of boxes away.

As he wondered about their history, the ship began to move, no sounding horn to see it off. Yohan carefully lifted the tarp to see his homeland drifting farther and farther away. As the sun rose, he wondered if it would still be there for him to come back to when everything drew to a close.

* * *

This is a fictional story based on five visual prompts.

All viewpoints are my own!

CHAPTER TWO

The Twin Notions of Patriotism and Nationalism

This essay discusses the notions of the nation, patriotic sentiments, and related subjects.

The words nationalism and patriotism are both quite commonplace in everyday Indian vocabulary. Both patriotism and nationalism reinforce a strong sense of pride and identity in one's country.

But, there is a minute distinction between the interchangeably used words. The origins of both words come from the Greek and Latin language families. The Greek "*patris*" refers to the fatherland, while the French "*patriote*" denotes fellow countrymen. Patriotism refers to a sense of pride with regard to one's country. Patriots feel joy for the accomplishments of their home base while acknowledging its shortcomings. Usually, soldiers or those involved in governmental sectors are referred to as patriots - although even you and I can be classified as the same.

Paraphrasing from G. Schochet's essay, patriotism is the political counterpart to the saying "*blood is thicker than water*". It translates to the fact that we put family, or our brethren, in front of all else. People of a particular country are bound together by an invisible contract to foster a sense of protectiveness due to their being alike.

The Latin "*natio*" refers to birth. Nationalism is an extreme form of patriotism where one believes in the utmost superiority of their nation. There is no objectivity - nationalism eradicates the idea of there being a detrimental action. This means a prevalent group exists that is disinterested in further development. They believe that their country is inferior to none. An almost obsessive attitude is developed, where a slight criticism is viewed as a threatening attack on the government in charge. This is quite a dangerous attitude to have, and enough of these voices can make a country liable to dictatorship or absolute rule.

Sydney J Harris, a prominent American journalist, famously stated,

"The patriot is proud of his country for what it does, and the nationalist is proud of his country no matter what it does."

Both patriotism and nationalism establish a sense of belonging. This sense of belonging is established through common tokens. Flags and national mottos are used almost uniformly among countries. One relates to a greater congregation of people when they see the tri-color flag or the emblem of four lions, rather than other localized manifestations of community.

The French Renaissance and the American independence struggle strongly shaped the initial concept of nationalism. It was meant to be a representation of Western liberalism and democracy - in short, nationalism meant the urge to work for collective welfare.

However, in recent times, one associates nationalism with the aforementioned negative connotations. This connotation includes conscious exclusion and policies of isolation. In the name of love for one's country, those of different racial origins, immigrants, and members of other countries are discriminated against. One places importance only on the interests of his own country as opposed to international cooperation.

Many academics like George Orwell and Rabindranath Tagore voiced their qualms with nationalism. On the last day of the 19th century, Tagore wrote the poem "The Sunset of the Century ."The theme was his critique of nationalism. One line sums up his views -

The naked passion of self-love of Nations, in its drunken delirium of greed, is dancing to the clash of steel and the howling verses of vengeance.

Jingoism, or aggressive foreign policy, is another form of nationalism - it advocates for war to preserve national interest. This jingoism is especially prevalent in fascist regimes to establish racial or ethnic superiority. An immediate example that comes to mind is Nazi Germany. The current Russian invasion of Ukraine is also one backed by nationalism. Russia's claim to Ukrainian territory is supposedly justified by the fact that the two countries were united under the Soviet Union, and thus are culturally related.

With reference to cultural ties, I would like to make yet another distinction between a country and a nation. Different sources have their own criteria for what constitutes a nation and a country. The commonly used Eurocentric view is as follows:

A nation is an abstract concept referring to a group of people united by culture. Culture includes language and value systems. However, others contest this view, stating that culture only signifies a social group and not a nation. That is, a nation has some political affiliation or another.

A country, on the other hand, is agreed upon as a geographically demarcated territory. The opinion that India is a country has existed for several centuries. The Greek Empire used the term Indica. Emperor Ashoka used Jambudvipa, and the Chinese referred to the South Asian subcontinent as Indu. But the concept of India as a nation, many believe, arrived with the East India Company. The idea of nationhood for India was not born out of cultural similarities - instead, it was from the joint struggle against colonialism. The independent nation soon set up a democratic electoral system, which ties in with the use of "Republic" in the Republic of India.

Ironically, the democratic system has been challenged since the Declaration of Independence. A recent survey showcased that 55% of Indians advocated for authoritarian rule. This relates to the previous point, where states with charged national energy are extremely susceptible to dictatorial governments. Many have also been vocal about support for army rule, stating that these so-called 'patriots' would have the nation's best interests in mind.

It is essential to think of a few questions relating to patriotism and the starting ideals of nationalism. Does the country deserve the respect it demands in the form of patriotic sentiment? Is the definition of a nation constrained to men, or does it include ecology and other voiceless beings?

Does a member of a nation or country have to acknowledge national tokens as part of their individual identity?

Should one be shamed for not wanting to be involved in national events like Independence Day celebrations?

Raja Rammohan Roy stated that Indians could not be patriotic, as their main loyalties lay with caste. So, when one identifies as a patriot, where do their loyalties lie - to the people around them, to politicians, or configured systems and ideals?

To conclude, the line between patriotism and nationalism is not clearly demarcated. While translating our thoughts into words, our choice of words and attitude give us away.

One should be aware of the closely related schools of thought, what the schools stand for, and thereby what they themselves stand for.

CHAPTER THREE

Authoritarianism in Uganda Under IDI Amin

Authoritarianism is described by Oxford Languages as

"the enforcement or advocacy of strict obedience to authority at the expense of personal freedom."

The world is currently seeing an increase in authoritarian modes of governance. This is not the introduction of a new concept but merely the resurgence of a previous trend.

A recent survey conducted among Indians on the preferred type of government showed that the majority surveyed (55%) preferred an autocratic/authoritarian government.

Having a single ruler or government body to care for a country's affairs does not necessarily make it bad. Most dictatorships show more economic growth than democratic ones. Politicians and especially regional leaders use this single fact to show the extent of beneficence brought about by dictatorships or authoritarian regimes.

The reason why most dictatorships have better economies is not a secret. Power consolidated in the hands of a single person makes it far easier to make decisions and go through legal procedures. There is no legality of or even need to consult other people.

Countries with long-standing democracies are slowly but surely succumbing to the poison of power. Dictatorships give complete control of and access to any type of resources in the presiding area. Moreover, intercountry or even intercontinental politics can aid in ensuring the support of the general public.

Political repression, such as through censorship, is widely used to achieve the status of superintendence. The Internet is one tool that is aiding megalomaniacs. In this day and age, spreading disinformation is extremely easy. Since sources are varied and hard to trace for the layman, one believes that whatever he reads is the truth. He falls prey to a carefully crafted narrative and is not aware of the actuality of events. Covering up incidents and internal politics was easier in the twentieth century. This was done by strictly controlling newspapers and other accessible media of the time, like the radio and international reporters.

Idi Amin Dada Oumee, or simply Idi Amin, was the third president of Uganda in West Africa. He ruled the country from 1971 to 1979 and is deemed as one of the most brutal dictators of the twentieth century, along with his European counterparts. This essay examines how Idi Amin Dada took complete control of Uganda.

Idi Amin was born to tribal parents in the small Ugandan town of Koboko, roughly 540 km from Kampala, the country's capital. Although historians do not have a consensus on the year of his birth, most believe him to be born in 1925. Aspects of his childhood and early life are also speculations. His mother is said to be Assa Aatte, a herbalist of the Lugbara tribe. His father is assumed to be a Muslim Ugandan from the Kakwa tribe, who went by the name Amin Dada.

Amin joined the army around the age of 20. Enlistment was a huge refuge for the eldest sibling of a poor Ugandan family. He started as an assistant cook for the King's African Rifles. Sources differ as to what happened next. Some say Amin joined the war as part of the Burma campaign [1944-45], while others say he was only formally enlisted in 1946. After enlistment, he rose up the ranks to become one of the few Ugandans to achieve the coveted officer position before Ugandan independence.

Idi Amin became closely affiliated with Milton Obote, who would become the first president and prime minister of independent Uganda in 1962. Known as Obote's right-hand man, Amin soon became chief of the army and air force, wielding formidable power.

In 1964, Uganda's second city, Jinja, faced an unprecedented uprising against the 1st Battalion of the Ugandan Army. Obote turned to the British for help. However, their response took too long to reach the country. By then, Obote had sent Defense Minister Felix Onama to negotiate with the mutineers. This step was later criticized as a hasty decision since Onama was held hostage by the mutineers who put forward extreme ultimatums.

The 'requests' included a steep increase in army wages and unchecked promotion of army candidates. Many sources feel that Amin is specifically included in this condition. A few years later, Amin organized a military coup against Obote. Obote had left the country in Amin's hands when he left to attend a Commonwealth conference in Singapore in 1971.

Reports say that Obote's relationship with Western leaders was strained at the time and thus alludes to the probability of Western participation in the same event. Obote's fall from the 'throne' was considered a celebratory event, especially as Amin followed him.

Idi Amin's tribal heritage played an integral role in his usurpation of the position of president of Uganda. Godrey Lule was Uganda's former Minister of Justice and Constitutional Affairs under Amin. According to him, "The system Amin [has] built up reflects his own background and peculiar talents." The Kakwa tribe was not a majority tribe in Uganda - it had a greater presence in places like Southern Sudan. Many Sudanese people lived in Uganda at the time, making up the 'Nubian' community/population. The Nubians/Sudanese were fiercely loyal to Amin, who bought their loyalty with luxury goods.

CIVIL LIBERTIES AND CONSTITUTIONAL RIGHTS

Amnesty International made a detailed report regarding the status of civil liberties and constitutional rights in authoritarian Uganda. They were concerned with the recent introduction of repressive laws that subjugated Ugandans.

The Ugandan parliament was dissolved, and plainclothes officers were given the power to determine whether everyday subjects were to be left alive or killed. Courts and the Ugandan press were ironically under full control of the executive, who made impulsive decisions.

Several security organisations, including the Public Safety Unit and the State Research Bureau reported directly to Amin. With 10,000 recorded killings in the first year of his regime, many Ugandans fled to neighbouring countries or went into hiding to escape the atrocities being committed in front of their eyes.

Many prominent figures of Uganda lost their lives in carefully engineered 'accidents'. These include Chief Justice Benedicto Kiwanuka and Anglican archbishop Janani Luwuum. A report by the New York City Bar Association's Committee on International Human Rights estimated that between 100,000 and 500,000 people became victims of Amin's reign of terror.

Following are two of the more prominent decisions taken during Amin's rule that greatly affected Uganda as well as the world outside of it.

ASIAN EXPULSION

Amin quickly established the direction of his rule to negate any doubts about his actual intentions. He did so by targeting the Asian diaspora of Uganda in 1972. South Asians had been sent to Uganda in 1888 as bonded labourers to build the railways. Similar to their work in the Indian subcontinent, the railways were meant to make supervision and subjugation easier for the colonizers, as well as to discourage local production.

It is important to note the reason he targeted the Asian community. Asians owned 90% of businesses run in Uganda, and also accounted for 90% of the country's tax revenue. Amin used this fact to fuel the pre-existing anti-Asian sentiments prevalent among Ugandans.

Ugandans were frustrated with the fact that they had no stake in their own economy. To make matters worse, western media continued to portray Ugandans as helpless, and in need of foreign intervention. Amin planned his move exactly when tensions between the Ugandans and Asians were at their highest, ensuring a positive response.

He accused the Asians of "milking Uganda's money" - essentially labelling them as migrant thieves. However, the outreach of his message was much more polished. Amin stated that God had revealed the following to him in a dream - that the Asians' main mission of building the railway was completed. It was now time for them to leave the country in the hands of the fully capable Ugandans.

Amin called it the 'War of Economic Independence', which was later termed as the Economic War. On Amin's orders, more than 50,000 Asians were forced to leave Uganda within the span of three months. Most travelled on the same railway that their ancestors had helped build.

This was a move that made him an extremely controversial figure. Outside of Uganda, Amin was termed a ruthless beast who only cared about homogeneity. Inside of Uganda, however, the story was completely different. Ugandans praised Amin as a 'true patriot' who had the nation's best interests at heart.

This notion was further popularised by Uganda's development under Amin in the social aspect, with the introduction of a great number of schools and hospitals open to the Ugandan public.

OPERATION ENTEBBE

In 1976, Amin declared himself president for life - the fulfillment of Amin's deepest political desire. 1976 saw the hijacking of an Air France plane travelling from Tel Aviv, Israel, to Paris, with an intermediate stop at Athens. On 27th January 1976, passengers aboard Flight 139 were held hostage by two German and two Palestinian terrorists. The plane landed in Libya for a refill before reaching its new destination at Entebbe, Uganda.

This incident was later given the infamous name of "Operation Entebbe", or codename Operation Thunderbolt, by the IDF (Israeli Defense Forces).

The sole demand of the terrorists was to release fifty-three pro-Palestine militant prisoners jailed in Israeli and European jails. The terrorists behind the attack on Flight 139 were sponsored mainly by none other than Idi Amin. This is one of the few recorded incidents where a dictator has openly sponsored political blackmail. Amin did not hide his pro-Palestinian sentiments and was extremely vocal about his hatred for Israel.

Amin praised Hitler for the mass genocide orchestrated by him against the Jews of Europe. He was quoted saying the following to the Secretary General of the United Nations. - 'Germany is the right place where, when Hitler was the Prime Minister and supreme commander, he burned over six million Jews. This is because Hitler and all German people knew that Israelis are not people who are working in the interest of the people of the world. That is why they burned the Israelis alive with gas in the soil of Germany.'

Although his anti-semitism was known to the world at this point, his backing of the hijacking still came as a surprise. Israel played a huge part in bringing him to his current position of absolute dictator. Israel had sought the help of multiple Arab and African countries in 1962, including Uganda, to fortify its borders. Military training, supply of arms, construction work, and agricultural technologies, among others, were offered in return by Israel.

The smooth sailing of Amin and Israel's relationship soon came to a rocky end, only a short while before the hijacking. When Israel refused to sell fighter planes to Amin, he broke off the alliance. This also soured Uganda's relationship with Great Britain. Amin then turned to Libya's Muammar Gaddafi for support. Gaddafi agreed to sell the jets to Amin on the condition that Uganda did not reconcile with Israel.

Israel's defence, the IDF (Israel Defense Forces) moved swiftly to save most of the passengers on board Flight 139. In the process, all four hijackers and 55 Ugandan soldiers were killed, with eleven of Uganda's airborne defences destroyed. Kenya, who sympathized with Israel, offered refuge to the passengers of the airline that made it out alive.

Enraged, Amin sent out orders to the Ugandan police forces to find and kill all Kenyans living in Uganda. 245 Kenyans were reported dead, with an estimated 3,000 fleeing to the neighbouring African countries.

The Ugandan-Tanzanian war, or the Liberation War of 1978-9 changed the future of West African politics. The end result was the disappearance of the little fraternity holding the western part of the African continent together. The animosity between Idi Amin and Tanzania's Julius Nyerere was an open secret. Nyerere despised Amin's regime as an Obote sympathizer.

1972 saw the Tanzanian invasion of southern Uganda by the exiled supporters of Obote, orchestrated by Nyerere. This further strained the relation between the two countries, which culminated in a huge border dispute. In 1978, Amin invaded Tanzania, declaring the annexation of all territory to the north of the Kagera River. The war is thus also called the Kagera War in Tanzania.

The invasion was enough to convince Nyerere that Amin posed a grave threat. After forcing the retreat of Ugandan soldiers from the area, Tanzania's military prepared for another invasion of their neighbour country. Figuring out their weak spots and working around them, the Tanzanians won a series of battles in the now-infiltrated south Uganda. Nyerere and the Ugandan exiles took over Kampala and introduced a new representative government in 1979. The end of the war was marked with the removal of Amin loyalists and Amin fleeing to Libya.

The representative government led by Godfrey Binaisa was removed in a coup. Milton Obote's return to the presidential position was marked with a series of rebellions.

As for Amin, his brief refuge in Libya allowed him to escape the African continent to Jeddah, Saudi Arabia. He passed away on foreign soil in 2003 due to kidney failure.

Amin was undoubtedly a force to deal with. People living in Uganda at the time either feared him, loved him, or both. Despite all the atrocities he has committed, he is looked up to as a 'true patriot' for opening up the Ugandan economy to his subjects. In a polarising manner, he is also seen as cunning for using people's weaknesses and disunity for his own political and personal gain.

With authoritarianism on the rise, as detailed in the introduction, it is time for us to step back and look at historical examples. Only by doing that can we be aware of the different stories that float around and decide for ourselves whether it is a good or a bad thing. **And whether it is a system one would want to be a part of...?**

ANALYSIS OF POPULAR MEDIA

CHAPTER FOUR

Notions of Gender in Popular Media

I explore the portrayal of gender and associated topics in popular media. Mainly, I highlight gender ideals, encouraged behaviour, and stereotypes. This has been done through three visual components/ video advertisements that I have analysed – and shared my viewpoints.

The three advertisements selected for analysis are:

1. **Seagram's Imperial Blue's "Men Will be Men": Anniversary edition [1]**
2. **Titan Raga's "#BreakTheBias" [2]**
3. **Gillette's "Is this the best a man can get?" [3]**

Keywords: Gender, Media, Advertisements, Gendered stereotypes, Gender ideals, Gender roles, Sex and Gender, Masculinity, "Boys will be boys", "Men will be men", Feminism, #MeToo Movement

Definitions and Dissection

Gender and sex have their roots in Old French, which comes from Latin.

Gender comes from 'genus' (Latin), meaning birth, family, or nation. The word sex comes from the Old French' sexus' or 'sexe'.

The two were used interchangeably in the 15th century. Majorly due to the 1970s Feminist movement, sex became associated with biological factors (hormones, reproductive organs), and gender assumed socio-cultural significance (behaviour, expression). [4] The usage of the word gender in this sense has risen considerably in the 21st century, reaching peak usage in 2019. [5] Additionally, it is now believed that gender has different manifestations and is not limited to the man-woman binary.

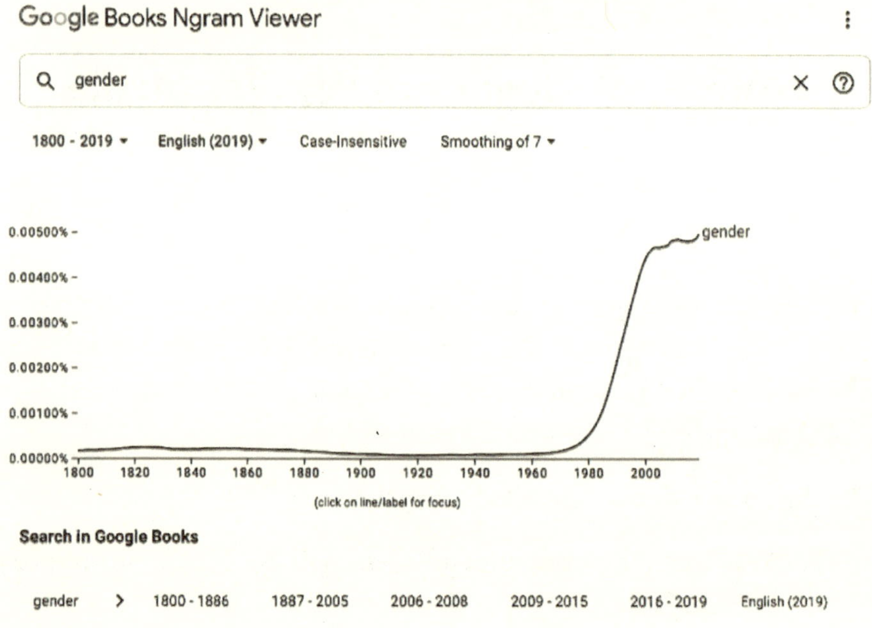

Terms like cisgender and non-binary appear much more frequently in visual media and popular culture, including the news, television shows, and social media platforms.

A "widely held, fixed, and oversimplified idea" is a stereotype. **[6]** Gender stereotypes portray ideas about a particular gender and are used to market products - called gendered marketing. For e.g., makeup products advertised to a teen female base and protein powder catered to teen males.

Gender stereotypes are represented in tandem, reinforcing each other - if men are strong and aggressive, women must be weak and passive; if women are emotional, men are stoic. [7]

AD 1: Seagram's Imperial Blue's "Men Will be Men": Anniversary edition [1]

A seller in a jewellery store shows a solitaire diamond ring to a customer. The customer looks tired, and his collars are loose - one might assume he has been drinking.

The customer asks for a bigger ring and is given a 1-carat diamond ring. When asked whether it is for a first wedding anniversary, he replies that it is their tenth. The seller congratulates his wife as a lucky one and provides a 3-carat ring. The seller asks when the anniversary is. The response states "yesterday," and the seller takes the ring back to provide a 5-carat ring.

The 'iconic' tagline of the brand then rings in, in a passive, almost encouraging tone: "Because Men Will Be Men." This advertisement was released in 2011 by Seagram's Imperial Blue, an Indian whiskey brand owned by Pernod Ricard, a French premium spirits company.

Social implications of the chosen components:

The first component is part of a 26-year-old marketing campaign that uses the tagline "Men Will Be Men." It was developed by the advertising company Ogilvy & Mather. It is important to note that liquor cannot be openly advertised in India.

In all ads of the campaign, men are portrayed as fickle, chasing after women's validation no matter the cost. Their embarrassing antics are counterproductive and are anything but gentlemanly but are viewed as 'fresh' humour. Response to the tagline has been overwhelmingly positive, especially online.

The founder of a business consultancy firm was quoted as saying:

"I can't understand why this should offend anyone. The ads don't portray women badly. They simply magnify how men behave around women." **[8]**

This ad, in particular, is slightly different from its peers, depicting a man forgetting his tenth wedding anniversary. The attempt to salvage the situation by buying an expensive ring showcases a shallow attitude towards one of the key people in his life. Therefore, the behaviour, paired with the tagline, cannot merely be written off as a joke.

The phrase is the main propeller of this agenda. "Men will be men" is closely associated with that of "Boys will be men." "Boys will be boys" initially dismissed young boys for being childish and engaging in fights. It has evolved to defend the predatory behaviour of adolescent boys towards women.

"Men will be men" takes it up a notch, excusing the actions of grown adult men. The phrase is not used to raise men up to a standard of celebrating their victories and achievements - it is used to bring them down to a group of undesirable attributes. **[8]**

5 Indian women working in advertising and marketing were interviewed about Imperial Blue's ad campaign. **[8]** Some responses garnered were:

"What is not okay, is their tagline - men will be men. We are so tired of being told that men are incapable of change and growth. I pity men who are told that they will remain that way.

We're begging for them to be better."

"Portraying women solely as objects of desire, and portraying men as (...) selfish and don't care about things that matter, is in poor taste towards both genders."

"While at one side, we fight for a #MeToo, we allow ourselves to applaud this ad without seeing the bigger problem."

*The founder of the business consultancy firm - quoted earlier - was a woman interviewed as part of this exchange.

AD 2: Titan Raga's "#BreakTheBias" [2]

Four business people - one woman and three men - are assessing a list of potential candidates for a promotion. The short-haired woman hands a recommended list to the man beside her.

He reads: "Kiran, recommended by Rajath. Of course."

He explains - Rajath has been singing the praises of Kiran, the company's young fresher. The two are always doing work together, even on weekends. Kiran is visualized as a young woman wearing tight clothes, high heels, and flirtatious smiles.

This imagination entertains those in the room. They decide to call Kiran to see if she matches up to their idea of her. Except, Kiran is a young man.

The ad ends with the phrase, ***"Change the way you look at a woman's success. She is unstoppable now."***

This advertisement, #BreakTheBias, was promoted by Titan Raga on Women's Day. Titan Raga is a watch company marketed towards women and belongs to the Titan Company Limited (part of the TATA Group).

ANALYSIS:

This video talks about women in the corporate sector. Women in managerial positions are assumed to have gained their standing through sexual favours, and not on their own.

In the video, the imagined Kiran wears fitted clothing and a lot of makeup.

These are viewed in India as Western trends - they rip away a woman's innocence by calling attention to herself. The only woman on the board of directors discussing this notion is a stark contrast.

She wears a sari, subtly shown as a sanskari woman who covers herself up in comparison to the 'modern' woman. She additionally has short hair, reinforcing the situation where corporate women adopt 'masculine' traits, such as short hair, to be taken more seriously by her [male] peers.

The ad was well-received by the general public, with many praising the company for being progressive. It is quite ironic, then, that these kinds of ads, built on a feminist or women-empowering narrative, are conveniently promoted only around Women's Day. It is worth noting that the #BreakTheBias hashtag has not been varied in any of their later campaigns despite the positive response it garnered.

A related point is also that all the products of Titan Raga are traditionally feminine - small and dainty watches covered in gemstones in 'feminine' colours such as rose gold. This does not necessarily reflect the company's stance on feminism but is an observation.

AD 3: Gillette's "Is this the best a man can get?" [3]

The advertisement begins with overlapping voices that speak about "bullying, the #MeToo movement against sexual violence…". This sets the overall tone for the advertisement, which attempts to bring another angle to its age-old tagline, "The Best a Man Can Get."

This narration is accompanied by short clips. At first, aggressive physical fighting, cyberbullying, and sexual harassment of women, including those in the workplace, are depicted. Then, male advocates for the #MeToo movement are shown, as are situations where men intervene to prevent other men from objectifying women.

The ad thus calls for the end of toxic masculinity and the departing of healthier ideals for young boys.

This ad was launched in 2018 by the shaving brand Gillette, owned by the company Procter & Gamble (P&G). It was directed by Somesuch, a UK-based production company known for its politically fueled ad campaigns.

ANALYSIS:

The third ad urges men to hold themselves to a higher standard, inspiring other men to do the same, for "the boys of today will be the men of tomorrow".

However, the campaign received intense backlash from its target audience - males from ages 12 and upwards. Many men were upset at the politicising of razors. Gillette lost nearly 30% of their customer base as a result of boycotts of Gillette and the parent company, Procter and Gamble (P&G). Dollar Shave Club was seen as the popular alternative.

The ad was interpreted as blanketing masculinity as bad. The general consensus was that Gillette was attempting to emasculate men by portraying them in an "amateurishly stereotypical" way, a "caricature of masculinity". **[10]**

This is significant as "Not All Men" was a standard response to those calling out sexual assault and rape through the #MeToo movement (which the ad supports). Additionally, the ad was called a 'virtue signal', and was accused of 'pandering to the feminists'.

P&G's global communications VP stated:(Paraphrased)

"We wanted to call out a few bad behaviours among good behaviours so that we can hold ourselves to a higher standard which is better for men, women, and society." **[11]**

Subconsciously, we are affected by catchy jingles and taglines in TV ads.

Repeated exposure reinforces certain ideals/behaviours that can negatively impact viewers - a connection was observed between the portrayal of men as unemotional with depression among young boys. [7]

Therefore, the portrayal of gender, gender ideals and behaviour - including the candid promotion of phrases such as 'Boys will be boys" or "Men will be men" - in accessible media is to be assessed more carefully than ever.

CHAPTER FIVE

The World Before Her: A Commentary of The Film

Disclaimer:

- Dialogues/ statements are paraphrased ones.
- I have taken the creative liberty of arranging certain events of the film non-sequentially to contribute to the overall flow of the essay, thus aiding my storytelling.
- This essay also documents my current personal views on the topic of feminism in India.

* * *

The World Before Her is a 2012 film by Nisha Pahuja, a Canadian Indian.

The film documents the supposedly contrasting lives of two women in India and thus attempts to make us redefine the meaning we assign to certain words.

These include "regressive and progressive", or "traditional and modern". Our ideals of freedom, independence and beauty in the present-day [Indian] society are also confronted head-on by the juxtaposition of stories.

One side of the story follows a woman named Prachi. As a trainer of the women's wing of a major Hindu extremist organisation*, Prachi takes a lot of pride in educating young girls about the ideals of the Hindutva movement during annual boot camps. She is direct in her approach and shows her loyalty to the group early on.

Prachi is also vocal about how she is nothing but a product created to pass down the core principles set by the organisation. Her father mentions that he would receive no greater joy than if Prachi died for the Hindutva cause. It is important to note that her father, a part of the overall movement, sent Prachi to these boot camps as a child.

Although not the headliner of these camps, Prachi is an important authoritative figure. She is of the strong belief that girls should learn to defend themselves instead of doing "girly things". Femininity is treated as a coin; one side is vehemently demonised, while the other is praised, although some might prefer the word 'imposed'. Masculinity, meanwhile, is associated with physical strength and undulating power. Passion is put on a pedestal for the same audience.

This is a common thread within the organisation, with some prominent members playing one extreme or the other. The head of Durga Vahini was recorded speaking to the attendees during a meeting and shamed the 'modern' women of India for wearing skimpy clothing. She, and most others, felt that this was against the culture of India. According to them, a woman's role is to maintain her sanctity until a socially approved union takes place. "A woman's body is a temple" is thus taken in a quite literal sense.

Great importance is also assigned to the role of marriage in a woman's life. The same head was heard stating that a girl was to 'be married before she

---

* The Vishva Hindu Parishad and its factions are based on the idea of Hindutva, or Hindu supremacy, specific to the Indian region. Bajrang Dal (Brigade of Hanuman) is the youth branch of the Vishva Hindu Parishad. Durga Vahini (Army of Durga) is the female counterpart of Bajrang Dal, aimed at girls of ages 12-18.

was too old to be tamed'. Thought is thus explicitly stated as a danger, a threat to the integrity of the cause. Members are brought up to be sheep, ready to risk their lives for the cause of a movement in the hopes of being defined as devoted individuals. Loyalty goes beyond the self and for the sake of a better future.

* * *

The 'other world' that is exposed to us in the film follows a young woman named Ruhi. Her ultimate dream is to win the Pantaloons Femina Miss India contest by bagging the Miss India crown. However, this is not a dream special to her. It is one present in the minds of the thousand other participants.

The film takes us on the journey of how contestants are chosen through a process of elimination. The contestants are taught fitting mannerisms to better their chances of winning the crown. This training includes how to walk appealingly and how to win over the judges with politically correct answers to their disjointed questions. Additionally, the woman in charge of training mentioned that participants had to be prim and proper, as expected of factory products, an interesting parallel to the statement by Prachi.

The candidates, self-claimed 'modern women', all talk of how they are independent. According to them, it is their choice to take part in the pageant and showcase how beauty is not necessarily vanity. But it is quite evident that their independence banks on constant pandering to the 'other'. The male gaze* is not only a normalised reality but a stamp of approval, a bar to surpass expectations.

These women step out of their comfort zone to achieve the superficial goal of being the most beautiful woman of the year. As an example,

* The male gaze, according to feminist theory, talks of the sexualised portrayal of women in media. Men look at women's bodies as objects that are to be dominated or lorded over as they are "weaker in nature".

one participant verbalises her discomfort in wearing a bikini during an evaluation. However, she states that she has to go through it in the face of the bigger picture.

Another woman is coerced into undergoing the process of injecting Botox* into her face. Her verbal protests are ignored; the surgeon states that she will not leave until the girl has had the botox procedure*. Her chin is apparently disproportionate compared to the rest of her face - a feature so jarring that it is invisible to everyone but the surgeon herself.

It translates into a different, albeit loosely related argument had the contestant chosen this for herself. However, she did not. The decision was forced upon her by an external and fabricated by the same as if it really was her choice all along.

A further infuriating proceeding during the pageant preparation is carried out by the male evaluator. His job is to decide whether the contestants have enough sex appeal to make the effort to enter the competition, let alone win. His (un)solicited advice is not restricted to the elimination period of determining participants. It extends to every session organized for women.

He teaches the women to pose 'properly' in order to draw in the male audience and, thus, influence the judges' decision. However, a woman's worth is not just determined by her face; it is imperative to note that her legs are also of equal importance. Therefore, the evaluator organises a 'leg photoshoot', where these women are made to wear bed sheets over their upper body to showcase the "seductive nature of a woman's legs".

Beauty pageants, marketed as being 'for the modern-day woman', contain close to nothing in terms of awareness of the struggles that women face in

---

* Facial botox (toxin injections) constitute a procedure which paralyses face muscles, stopping wrinkles from forming. Although it is a temporary procedure lasting 3-4 months, it entails numerous health complications. These include muscle weakness and difficulty in swallowing. Recently, a trend of injecting botox for aesthetic reasons has developed to appear more youthful.

everyday life. Moreso, the pageants themselves add salt to the wound by formulating the perfect woman and capitalising off of peoples' insecurities.

Up till this point, the two sides were shown as synchronous but detached. One scene in the film showcases protests against the Miss India beauty pageant. Protestors included many Indian laymen, as well as some women from Durga Vahini. Notably, one woman in the crowd was carrying a placard stating that women are not to be objectified and beauty is not to be quantified by a "perfect face/body".

In both stories, there is one constant: Young girls are indoctrinated to induce divisions in everyday society without inhibition. It becomes a subconscious effort, one that is not given too much thought.

In the case of the boot camp, religious dividends are introduced. To be associated with a Muslim or Christian is blasphemous. Similarly, the beauty industry nitpicks every aspect of a girl until she succumbs to vain, capitalistic intent. Girls are treated as toys to be experimented with. Frustrations are projected onto one another, creating unnecessary animosity between people facing the same struggles. Both sides thus prey on the impressionability of young minds; to go to an extreme, one might even say that they are being brainwashed.

Internalised misogyny also plays an incremental and intertwined role. It has fully taken over the lives of these women, as well as those outside their social circle; broadly, it impacts all women in India. This is a notion supported throughout the film by its protagonists, who constantly pit themselves against one another, be it in terms of beauty, intelligence, or other comparable factors - and not just within the pageant.

Neither groups of women are able to look at their viewpoints objectively. Within the film, value systems are distorted and shoeboxed to fit into certain unattainable ideals. While this action is quite striking for viewers, it seems transparent, even nonexistent to the doers themselves.

So-called 'modern' women use Westernization as an escape, while the 'traditional' women use outdated cultural principles and practices to do the same. In essence, they are not as different as they try to portray themselves. Both groups are trying to escape from the shackles imposed on them by society. But, they fail to realise that they now enter looser shackles voluntarily; and this is what they consider freedom. This illusion of independence has taken control, blinding them to the fate they now face.

While this documentary may have come out 11 years ago, its relevance in current Indian society is one that is alarming. To see that we have not changed our mindsets in the slightest over a decade means stagnation in our ideals and the notable absence of its re-evaluation.

Hopefully, as more notice is brought to this issue within the feminist movement in India, we will make a more concentrated effort to prevent the fossilisation of our thought process and the harm it entails.

CHAPTER SIX

Thinking Like a Mountain: An Analysis

The essay "Thinking Like A Mountain" by Aldo Leopold talks of alternative thinking. This term is not being used in the casual manner of discovering or creating a new invention or spurring modern change. Leopold begins his essay in an unorthodox fashion - by introducing the howl of a wolf. This howl does not seem all that special until we unearth the story behind it.

The howl means something different to each ear it reaches. It means trouble for both the deer and the hunter and means bloodshed and sleeplessness to the forest around. However, not many know that the mountain on which all this takes place has its own viewpoint.

The author himself only realises this at a later stage in his life. It was common to hunt wolves - lesser wolves meant more deer, and more deer meant more for hunters as well as to sustain nature. The reality was not as idealistic as humans, however. The wolves kept the deer population in check, thus allowing for the flora of the mountain to continue sustenance. Lesser wolves meant a rapid growth in deer, and the mountain, whose forest once boasted lush greenery and exotic varieties of local shrubs and plants, has turned into a barren wasteland.

Humans can easily turn to another mountain to continue their unchecked intrusion of nature. But the mountain alone mourns the loss of its once unquantifiable beauty.

Objectively speaking, the correlation that killing wolves will lead to prosperity for everyone involved is a reasonable initial thought. As exemplified in the last paragraph of Leopold's essay, there exists a consensus regarding a worthwhile life. It requires us to be safe and secure and to live long with all the luxuries one could possibly have.

A life led in this manner is considered the peak of success as well as peace. The methods used to achieve this stability in life vary since it is extremely personal and, therefore, subjective. It is quite interesting to see, therefore, that the author adds one more adjective to describe this so-called 'prized' experience: dullness.

Dullness is used concerning the fact that such a life poses no need to exert ourselves, neither mentally nor physically. It dictates our bodies to waste away until we are indistinguishable from a vegetable or potato sack. We are, by the end of things, as barren and lifeless as the mountain without its forests. This Act is blindly termed as a 'safety precaution' which is quite ironic - we are not to determine what is to be saved or not. Upsetting the natural balance of things, whether in the jungle or outside, leads only to decrepitude, however slowly it progresses.

It does not come as a surprise that humans are inherent megalomaniacs. Attaining power is, nonetheless, only one of the many desired outcomes. Control is a very important factor in this discussion. People love to control things. While ideas of fate, destiny, and divine providence are comforting, they do not give us the space to explore and come to conclusions by ourselves.

To abandon these predetermining ideas in favour of authority is an easy decision. Having a monopoly over the variables at play gives us a false sense of security, assuring us of a positive, desired outcome. This leads to a discord between the capability or potential of man versus that of nature. Humans are indoctrinated to believe that commodities from the environment around us are ours to take by employing force and to use for our benefit - a forlorn justification for humans' exploitative nature.

The essay tries to inform the readers of this viewpoint - since we are introduced to this idea from a young age, we may not be aware of the fact that we think in this way. Awareness alone is of practically no use to people, apart from tapping into their conscience. One can simply read his essay and continue with the familiar, usual activities of everyday life. It is, after all, much easier to do than the alternative - to consider the weight of the actions that have been carried out for time immemorial.

Leopold brings this to the attention of the readers through the use of a quote. Henry Thoreau is quoted for a famous saying taken from one of his essays. It states –

"In wildness is the salvation of the world."

It is important here to note the distinction between wildness and wilderness. Here, wildness is not used as an indicator of reversion to animalistic behaviour. It is, instead, a symbol for tapping into the thought process and supposed sentience of other beings going through our cataclysm. Leopold's use of the quote elaborates on his previous point of thinking like a mountain.

The mountain knows that the wolf is important for its own well-being. It thus does not interfere with the ordinary cycle of birth and death that takes place in both the communities of the deer and the wolf. By thinking like the mountain, we can open our minds to the simple fact that we need not always be in control for things to operate smoothly. This obsession to always dominate and command is corrupting us and carving us out as stone-hearted, selfish and unempathetic people.

This realisation may surprisingly not bother many. For many people, the thought of being judged with the use of the adjectives above does absolutely nothing in terms of interruption of daily living. The only thing that matters is the peace in their own life.

A hunter requires his traps and poisons to be effective so that he can earn a living wage. A politician uses his sweet, sugar-coated words while running for office - and security for him is being able to hold onto the position he has fought so hard for. The common man is also concerned with this matter of feeling safe. He uses currency and suffrage to have a stake in the outcome of the immediate environment around him. Everyone, thus, actively plays a part in securing the dream life for themselves. And this is done with active disregard towards the resources used to achieve our destination.

To have lofty ambitions is an admirable trait. To have those ambitions at the cost of something much greater is alarmingly grave.

Although it is far beyond 'late', it is still worth a try to change our ways of interacting with the world around us.

The entire essay is, thus, a heavy and direct indicator that there is no real necessity for us to control and lord over all that we set our eyes on.

CHAPTER SEVEN

The Curious Relationships of the Dog in the Day Time: Analysis

An analysis of the book:

"THE CURIOUS INCIDENT OF THE DOG IN THE NIGHT-TIME"

BY MARK HADDON

***PwD = Person with Disabilities**

This essay is my review/analysis of a book.

BOOK: THE CURIOUS INCIDENT OF THE DOG IN THE NIGHT-TIME

AUTHOR: MARK HADDON

YEAR: PUBLISHED IN 2003, SET IN LATE 1990s

Abstract: This essay elaborates on topics of a family (Christopher's relationship with his father), Autism Spectrum Disorder/ ASD (Christopher and Asperger's Syndrome), as well as education for children with disabilities.

Summary of the book

The story is narrated in the first person by Christopher Boone, a 15-year-old with a photographic memory. Although it is not stated explicitly, the story hints at Christopher being on the Autism Spectrum. Specifically, Christopher having Asperger's Syndrome.

He lives with his father in the English town of Swindon, and the story is set in the late 90s. One day, Christopher finds his neighbour's poodle Wellington dead on the lawn. Despite discouragement from his father, Christopher is determined to find out who murdered Wellington and why.

He begins writing a book about the same, which takes the form of The Curious Incident of the Dog in the Night-time. Going out of his comfort zone, he interacts with residents of the neighbourhood to find possible clues for the murder and the motive behind it. While investigating Wellington's death, Christopher discovers that his neighbour, Mr Shears, had had an affair with his mother, whom Christopher had presumed dead.

He absentmindedly leaves his book on the dining table one day, where his father discovers it. Enraged that Christopher did not heed his advice, his father throws the book away. Desperate to get the book back and finish his investigation, Christopher searches for the book within the house. While doing so, he comes across letters in his father's room addressed to him from his mother. This leads to the discovery of a much more complex plot; It becomes something bigger than the death of a dog. His mother is not dead and never has been. The letters document the 'new' life that his mother leads with Mr Shears in the bustling city of London. His mother also asks Christopher to respond repeatedly, unaware of the fact that his father hid the letters.

Christopher's father had lied to him, telling him that she had died of a heart attack. Upon finding out that Christopher knew the truth, his father attempted to justify his actions. He wanted to avoid complications by mentioning his mother abandoning them. He then confesses to killing Wellington in a fit of rage after a fight with Mrs Shears, his lover. Christopher now feels unsafe around this man who has lied to him not only about his mother but also about murder.

Referring to the address in the letters, he decides to live with his mother in London instead. He takes on a terrifying journey, learning how to navigate a place entirely new, losing his pet rat, and dealing with the police to finally reach his destination. His arrival is met with surprise. Christopher's mother is elated to see her son after so long, but Mr Shears does not share the same sentiment. He is unwilling to adapt or give more attention to Christopher and his disability. Christopher's presence causes such a problem that his mother decides to leave Mr Shears and return to Swindon with Christopher. They move into a new apartment with his father visiting regularly. Christopher's pet rat (which he finds earlier) dies, and his father gives him a dog to cope with the loss. The novel ends somewhat abruptly, leaving readers with a feeling of incompleteness. Christopher receives an A grade on his A-Level Maths exam, the highest score. He plans to take his physics A-Levels the following year and attend a university in a different town. He claims that he can do so since he solved the mystery of Wellington's murder, travelled across to find his mother, and wrote a book documenting the entire process.

Social ecology

"The Curious Incident of the Dog in the Night-time" is set in the late 1990s in Swindon, United Kingdom. There are some clues that the book gives us to place the story in time.

- Christopher references many famous movies of the 80s. These include the 1982 science fiction movie Blade Runner (CH 229, Pg 242) and 1987's Star Trek: The Next Generation (CH 163, Pg 147).
- There are many references in CH 233.

Christopher plays Minesweeper, a game released in 1989. (Pg 253)

He also plays the game The 11th Hour, released in 1995. (Pg 259)

Christopher's mother, Judy, reads a documentary of Princess Diana titled "DIANA Her True Story" by Andrew Morton. She also reads the book "Rivals" by Jilly Cooper. These books were published in 1992 and 1988, respectively.

The author graduated from the University of Oxford in 1981 with a degree in English Literature. After graduating, he worked closely with children and adults with mental and physical disabilities, including autism. His experience taking care of PwDs would go on to influence his literary writing, as seen in 'The Curious Incident of the Dog in the Night-time'.

We encounter many social problems/phenomena in "The Curious Incident of the Dog in the Night-time." Some of these are discussed below.

Christopher and his father

The social and applied human sciences have been built upon the assumption that the "normal" family consists of a first-marriage conjugal couple cohabiting with biological children. (Canetto SS, National Library of Medicine)

When viewing Christopher's family as an outsider, they fit this definition. However, the relationships that the members of this family share are complex, with many underlying layers. Let us look at the relationship that Christopher shares with his father.

Christopher and his father, Ed, had a very close yet complex relationship with each other. Christopher heavily depends on Ed for social cues, which he is slow to pick up on. He and his father are quite similar in the sense that they both have few friends/confidants. Christopher tells everything about his life to his schoolteacher, Siobhan. The only person Ed is mentioned to be friends with is his co-worker, Rhodri. Ed himself tells Christopher that, "I mean, we're not that different, me and you." (CH 167, Pg 151)

It is a common trait to be disconnected from feelings most of the time for those having Asperger's Syndrome. Christopher prefers to think about things in a logical sense over an emotional one, which can make it hard for people to understand or empathise with him.

For example, he does not get upset when he finds out from Mrs. Alexander (his neighbour) that his mother, Judy, had had an extramarital relationship with Mr. Shears. He retells his conversation to his teacher, Siobhan. She asks him, "Did it make you upset to find out that your mother and Mr Shears had an affair?". To this, Christopher responds, "...I don't feel sad about it. Because Mother is dead. And because Mr Shears isn't around anymore. So I would be feeling sad about something that isn't real and doesn't exist. And that would be stupid." (CH 109, Pg 94-95)

On the flip side, Ed struggles with the multitude of feelings washing over him. He cannot bring himself to share his feelings so openly. In particular, Ed struggles with telling Christopher the truth about his mother. Judy runs away with Mr Shears, and Ed, in a fractured mental state, tells Christopher that she has died of a heart attack. Since he is already in pain, he could not bear the thought of his son disregarding the situation as 'something that has happened'. He is ashamed of what has taken place and is also afraid that Christopher will choose his mother over him after finding out the truth.

One of the many roles played by Ed is that of a father. However, his role now has a stigma attached to it since Christopher's mother is absent from the picture. Ed is henceforth not a father but a 'single' father. Society looks very harshly upon those who do not fit the ideal of a modern nuclear family. Bringing up a child alone is looked down upon by both men and women. (The task of bringing up a child is primarily viewed as a woman's job. Even in modern society, fathers participating in raising the child are sometimes referred to as 'babysitters'.)

Thus, Ed is not only worried about raising Christopher but also about what the rest of society will think about his failed marriage. Although marriage is currently viewed as a mere civil contract in the Western world, Ed will be blamed for not being able to keep his family together.

In most cultures, it is considered normal for the man to express anger - it is even encouraged. But according to Christopher, Ed was not a hot-headed person. Ed is described as a calm person who rarely gets angry. The same behaviour is reflected in Christopher, who only gets mad if his physical space is interrupted. However, when Ed finds the book documenting Christopher's investigation, his fear takes the form of anger. Ed does not want Christopher to find out that he murdered Wellington. Ed goes ballistic and screams expletives at Christopher.

“Father had never grabbed hold of me like that before. (...) But Father is a more level-headed person, which means he doesn’t get angry as quickly and he doesn’t shout as often.” (CH 127, Pg 103)

Many parents don’t mean to silence their children, but they don’t know what to do with their anger other than to act as though everything is fine. They can successfully silence their children because of the power they wield.

One of the definitions of power given by Weber is - “the ability to control the behaviour of others, even in the absence of their consent.” Since the family is the smallest social unit, the power exerted by its primary (usually older) members is informal yet binding.

Here, Ed holds positional power, i.e., his position as a father demands reverence from his child. Children in families grow up to understand, through socialisation, that they are subordinate to their parents. Additionally, the father’s word is taken more seriously than the mother’s in a ‘traditional’ patriarchal family.

Ed’s nightmare comes to life when, later in the book, Christopher finds a pack of letters from his mother addressed to him. Christopher feels so disconnected from reality that he ceases to respond to his father’s anxious cries, even when Ed tries to touch him to clean him up.

“And I didn’t scream. And I didn’t fight. And I didn’t hit him…” (CH 157, Pg 144)

Ed tries to explain the situation, stating - “I did it for your good, Christopher. Honestly I did. I never meant to lie. I just thought…I just thought it was better if you didn’t know (...) I was going to show them to you when you were older.” (CH 157, Pg 143)

He then confesses to killing Wellington in a fit of rage. With so much pent-up anger, and against so many people, Wellington only acted as a trigger for Ed.

"And all I could think of was that she (Mrs Shears) cared more about this bloody dog than she did about you or me. And it was like everything I'd been bottling up for two years just..." (CH 167, Pg 152)

He hopes that by revealing all the truths, his son will stay by his side. However, this ends up having the opposite effect, where Christopher trusts him less after finding out the truth.

"I had to get out of the house. Father had murdered Wellington. That meant he could murder me because I couldn't trust him, even though he had said, 'Trust me', because he had told a lie about a big thing." (CH 167, Pg 152-153)

Although it is never stated explicitly, many of the behavioural issues exhibited by Christopher are synonymous with those on the Autism Spectrum. Some include that he dislikes being touched, has a distaste for certain colours (yellow and brown), and smashes things when he is angry or upset.

Most children with Asperger's Syndrome have a difficult time relating to others socially. Their behaviour and thinking patterns are also usually rigid and repetitive. Let us see how this plays into his behaviour at school, with his teachers and peers.

The following lines heavily imply that Christopher attends a special school for those with disabilities.

"All the other children at my school are stupid. Except I'm not meant to call them stupid, even though that is what they are. I'm meant to say that they have learning difficulties or that they have special needs. But this is stupid because everyone has learning difficulties (...)

But Siobhan said that we have to use those words because people used to call children like the children at school *spaz* and *crip* and *mong*, which were nasty words. But that is stupid too because sometimes the children from the school down the road see us in the street when we're getting off the bus, and they shout, 'Special Needs! Special Needs!'." (CH 71, Pg 56)

1990s UK saw the rise of awareness about autism and the spectrum. On the flip side, it also saw the rise of ableist slurs and hate crimes committed against those on the spectrum.

Christopher mentions, "Terry, who is the older brother of Francis, who is at the school, said (...) they didn't let *spazzers* drive rockets that cost billions of pounds (...) I'm not a spazzer, which means spastic, not like Francis, who is a spazzer..."

The words spaz, crip, and mong are highly offensive slurs against disabled persons.

"*Crip*" is North American slang used to mock one for not having limbs. It comes from the word 'crippled'.

"*Mong*" is a British term referring to those with learning difficulties, specifically Down Syndrome, in a derogatory manner. It is derived from the word 'Mongol', as people having Down syndrome have slanted eyes, similar to people of Mongol descent.

"*Spaz*" is a term derived from 'spastic', which refers to those affected by muscle spasms. The term came to be used as slang in the late 1960s, around 1965, to mean one that was (socially) inept.

Differently-abled people and their rights

It has been and is still a struggle for PwDs all over the world to secure their right to education. "Proper" special education was only introduced in 1944 in the United Kingdom. Currently, a child has SEN or Special Educational Needs if they have more difficulty in learning than the majority of children of the same age. Or if they have a disability, which makes it difficult for them to use the same facilities as other children.

What follows is a contrast to the state and quality of education presented to students/children with disabilities (given the historical context) and those available to them in modern-day society.

In 1943, Leo Kanner described those with autism as being unable to relate to themselves or others, with the term autism derived from the root auto for self.

People living in the 1940s-90s did not know much about autism or other mental disabilities other than the fact that it was 'not normal'. Many even believed that autism could be administered through vaccines - this belief is still widely held over the world, although it has been debunked several times.

Before certain laws were passed by the Legislation, children with disabilities were not allowed to attend normal schools. This was out of fear that they would pass on their 'disease' to the other children or influence them to 'act out'. Many children were also abandoned.

Families in this period who had children with disabilities moved downward in social status, were frowned upon, and were socially ostracized. Children with disabilities were religiously viewed as Satan's children and were a result of the parents' sins prior to childbirth. (...) Often, children were shipped off to institutions, which resembled prisons.

The 1913 Mental Deficiency Act required school boards to identify children who were 'defective' and send them to live in institutions.

The Mental Deficiency Act was followed by The Education Act of 1944.

The 1944 Education Act introduced selection by disability - children with disabilities [were] sent to 11 types of special schools depending on their impairment.

However, it was The Education Act of 1962 that made a huge difference - It ensured that children with special needs would not receive a subpar education because of their condition(s), be it mental or physical.

The Education Act of 1962 – required Local Education Authorities (LEAs) to provide students with grants for living costs and tuition fees. It placed a legal obligation on parents to ensure that children received a suitable education at school or otherwise – failure to comply could result in prosecution. It also made LEAs legally responsible for ensuring that pupils attended school.

Currently, it is the choice of the parents regarding the education of a child with disabilities. Legally, a 'normal' school cannot reject an applicant on the basis of disability.

The Legislation gives rights to children with SEN (Special Educational Needs) to be educated in mainstream schools where their parents want this, and the interests of other children can be protected. It also allows for the Education Authority to assess a child who has SEN.

Children with special needs are also protected legally in case of unfair discrimination in educational institutions, called 'disability discrimination.' An example of this would be refusing to allow a pupil with behavioural issues to attend an after-school club. The Equality Commission has also put guidelines in place to assist schools and universities to practice equality.

CONCLUSION

The novel explores many different themes that are universal in nature, including those of independence, coping with loss, and subjectivity (due to disability), along with the predominant concept of social disorder.

These are explored through the individual (Christopher) and his relation to the fairly conservative society around him while being neurodivergent. Culture provides behavioural patterns, but what about the people whose patterns are different?

Because of his condition, Christopher's interactions are very limited. There are only a few people, like his family and schoolteachers, that accommodate him well. Given the climate surrounding autism at the time, the same may not be applicable to the rest of society. Christopher's limited social interactions tell us of a potential future where his talents go to waste. People would not willingly give opportunities to a person they are unable to understand or relate to, especially if they need extra attention.

As a person, Christopher depends on logic for most of his reactions to situations. When he is told that his mother died of a heart attack, he immediately takes note of the fact that most heart attacks happen to old people - his mother was young. Society would not consider this a 'normal' emotional reaction to loss, but for Christopher, this is a form of gaining closure.

Christopher's condition causes him to see the world in an atypical way reliant on logic. Since the book is from his perspective, readers start to empathise with him - the book also strongly suggests that everyone, unlike Christopher, has a subjective point of view.

I took a psychological approach to review the book, which is an observation I realised much after I finished it.

This taught me to relate problems on a larger scale or a community level than specifically to the individual.

THE ENVIRONMENT

CHAPTER EIGHT

Rural Livelihoods: Is There a Future?

This essay reports a research study on using natural materials in rural livelihoods, their loss, and the consequences to artisans and the environment.

A recent trip to Kaigal, Andhra Pradesh, showed the bleak reality of traditional livelihoods in the face of modernisation.

At Kaigal, I had conversations with farmers regarding handicrafts, and the future of the industry.

The farmers are facing the struggle to earn a stable wage. Many common complaints emerged from the interviews.

Some had to give up education to support their parents on the field, being $7^{th}/8^{th}$-grade graduates. Others did not get to experience education at all. In earlier days, the community used to live together and help each other out. However, over time, divisions and differences between different farmer groups ultimately led to less labour and the lack of a strong support system.

This report lists the research work from primary and secondary research sources.

1. THE SPECIFIC GOAL of the study

Traditional livelihoods are being degraded through our disregard for the environment around us.

This study focuses on the use of various natural materials and how they support rural livelihoods. It further elaborates on the replacement of these natural materials with synthetic ones, and the effect it has on both people and their surroundings.

Since the usage of natural materials is declining, the focus includes the effects of industrialization. Emphasis is given to rural artisans and craftsmen from India.

2. DATA NEEDED/COLLECTED

ARTISANS

1. The various artisanal/traditional occupations that are seen in Tamil Nadu.
2. Statistics (average) of people employed [in India/TN] who depend on environmental resources/ employment generation.
3. Demography - average age and gender of artisans.
4. The average income of people employed. Is it enough to sustain themselves?
5. How are the artisans affected in terms of social status?
6. In this day and age, industrial products and processes are cheaper than handcrafted ones. Are artisans able to compete and live reasonable lives?
7. What are some challenges artisans face in a quickly industrialising country like India?
8. How do they see their future? What do their children think of their trade? Will it be continued?
9. Were these artisans employed elsewhere before taking up traditional arts and crafts? If so, what were they doing before?
10. How many days in a year are they employed? What do they do during the other seasons?
11. How do consumers like us benefit from local artisanship?
12. What are some organisations/ who are some people working towards reviving these sustainable traditions and products?

13. Are there any government schemes to alleviate the problem? What is/are the status of these schemes?

ENVIRONMENTAL

1. How is artisanal trade linked to the local environment?
2. Synthetic products are currently rising in popularity since they last longer than natural materials.

    a. What are some other advantages of using synthetic materials instead of natural ones?
    b. What livelihoods have been lost entirely because of this change?

1. Do many artisans continue using natural materials because of sentimental value? Or is there something else that stops them from switching to synthetics/plastics?

Does loss of biodiversity have any correlation to the decline in traditional livelihoods?

3. Rural livelihoods

The introduction talks about natural materials and rural livelihoods and how these traditions are being threatened.

Merriam-Webster dictionary defines a *livelihood* as a "means of support or subsistence". [1] In a village, a person's livelihood largely depends on their family. If one is born into a farming family, one will probably also become a farmer. Families practising artisanship tend to pass on techniques or trade secrets specifically to relatives. The future generations can then continue practicing the same work, ensuring the survival of the craft, and a stable livelihood. [2]

Indigenous people living in forests or villages close to forested land depend on the nature around them to sustain themselves. A traditional source of their livelihood is the materials they gather from their environment. These include gathering materials from the forest, like honey, herbal medicines, and non-timber forest products (NTFPs). The forest products are gathered in large amounts for both consumption and sale. [3]

People living in these rural areas are engaged in basketry, carpet making, beadwork, carpentry, wood carving, and so on. The main focus of handicrafts was to fulfill the immediate needs of local people. However, as the artistry began attracting visitors and tourists to these areas, they were commercialised. Many types of handicrafts are supported by the government for tourism and cultural preservation. [4]

India is especially vibrant in the cultural artifacts/handicrafts scene with its many different expressions of art. Even within one state, different art forms are brought to life with different mediums. Within Tamil Nadu, Tanjore painting, Kanjivaram silks, bronze ornaments, floor rugs [5], crafting Veenas (musical instruments), and stone-carving are major artisanal livelihoods. [6]

Local producers use the many natural materials in their immediate environment to sustain themselves. While this is the primary source of income for most, many rural people also learn the arts to bring in some extra cash apart from their primary work.

Bamboo handicrafts are made in West Bengal, Assam and Tripura. The various items made from it include baskets, dolls, toys, mats, jewellery boxes, and many more. Colourful paper is often used in North India (Delhi, Ahmedabad, Patna, Allahabad, etc.) to create papier mache dolls, along with lamp shades, decorative flowers, puppets, and hand fans.

The practice of woodcraft predates stone sculpture. Toys, axes, jewellery boxes, bangles, and vermillion/ sindoor/ kumkum boxes are crafted. Woodworks from Gujarat, Karnataka, Kerala, and Uttar Pradesh are well known for their distinctive style. [7]

Borassus flabellifer, or Palmyrah (Palm), is the state tree of Tamil Nadu.[8] It greatly empowers the concept of self-sustainability among rural people. Dry palm leaves that had fallen on the ground were picked up to create thatched roofing for mud houses and huts. Palm leaves are also historically significant. They were folded and used to scribe many important works of Tamil literature, including the Thirukkural written by Thiruvalluvar. [9]

However, as times have progressed, these natural materials are being misused with disregard for the lives they support and the art they create. Traditional livelihoods are on the brink of life, with no means of environmental or economic support.

As they grow older, these farmers worry about the longevity and survival of their occupations. Many in their families, especially the younger generation, have moved to places like Bangalore in search of work; they do not want to continue the traditional agricultural livelihood as there is no money or any sort of gain for them doing so. The farmers then expressed that while they worry about the future of farming, they do not want people to take up farming for the same reasons.

Challenges faced by the handicraft industry

The same can be said of the handicraft industry of the country. For a country as rich and culturally diverse as India, it would be easy to assume that the artisan industries stay thriving. However, there are multiple challenges faced by the handicraft industry. One is the domination of synthetics and plastics in the industrial market. These materials are cheap to produce and even cheaper to purchase.

Diwali/ Deepavali is one of India's most important festivals, celebrated all over the country with different names and origin stories but with the same festive fervour. The pre-festive mood would set in, with every family out shopping for the perfect earthen lamps to light up their homes. Before electricity, these lamps would light up the entire house. Even after the introduction of electricity, people would go out in droves to buy decorated lamps for the holiday season.

This festival season was one of the busiest for potters, as they would not only have to make huge batches of lamps but also paint or mould them differently to beat out the competition. Nowadays, customers prefer cheap electric lights and expensive decorative pieces manufactured in bulk. [10]

This greatly harms the lives of not just one or two, but entire families of potters scattered across the country.

This is a great example of how traditional livelihoods are slowly but surely going off the radar. Another hurdle faced by artisans is their income or lack thereof. Any person still employed in one of the professions is severely underpaid, and many are deep in debt. Artisans are not strangers to the term "loan." There have been multiple government initiatives to bring banks and low-interest loans to rural areas for a long time now. [11]

However, the capability of repaying the loan is doubted when it comes to artisans. [12] This seed of doubt between the institution and the individual leads artisans to rely on informal sources for loans. As local moneylenders seem more approachable and relatable, they borrow from them. But this is not the most viable option, as moneylenders are known to charge exorbitant interest rates. Debtors thus end up falling into a debt trap and are unable to escape it. [13]

The effort they put into their art is not appreciated, and yields very little money. They receive amounts that are not enough to sustain one person, let alone an entire family. As people abandon their livelihoods due to any of these various reasons, or all of them, the arts fade away until it is only 'once what was'.

4. **LEARNINGS** from the conversations

I contacted three resource persons that have ties to rural livelihoods.

- Mrs. Aparna Krishnan works closely with women who make cloth bags from the village Paalaguttapalle, Andhra Pradesh. She is one of the main efforts behind the #PaalaguttapalleBags effort.
- Ms. Kavitha Sridharan owns the jewellery company, Chingari, which frequently contacts people employed in rural livelihoods related to handicrafts, especially goldsmiths and weavers.
- Mr. Ananthoo runs OFM, or Organic Farmer's Market, which is concerned with organic agriculture/food.

Some traditional livelihoods include spinning and weaving, metalsmithing, goldsmithing, pottery, carpentry, handloom, embroidery and stone carving. This is generational work. Training is started to help the family business when the children are small - around the ages of 7 and 8. ***Due to the seasonal nature of some handicrafts, artisans take loans or work on other people's fields during the off-season.***

These occupations are becoming harder and harder to come by. Artisans believe that actual education is studying in the cities and not the learning of traditional handicrafts. The children are not being trained, and the show of interest is also extremely low. However, we don't have a moral right to expect children to continue the profession. Born and brought up in an artisan family, there will be nuances and things you pick up easily. ***But people will only take up something if there is a respectable economy behind it.***

Especially in this economy where prices are constantly increasing for all commodities, making money is the most important thing. ***People feel that they are wasting time by learning and implementing these skills when the outcome is less money for harder work*** - naturally, this is not a fancied combination.

No one buys from villages anymore, preferring cheap, factory produced products. This greatly demotivates artisans. Location is also an important factor. Artisans that are not concentrated in cities are usually hard to contact, on the rare occasion that somebody is interested in buying from them. ***No support system exists for them either.***

Industrial production is dominating because the cost - the damage to the environment and the livelihoods - is externalised. It is unaccounted for, making it seem inexpensive. However, if all these are factored in, industrial products would also be exorbitantly expensive.

Some are of the opinion that odd groups* cannot do anything about these fast-dying livelihoods. They believe that sustainable livelihoods will only be supported if pressure is put on the government.

Others feel that it has the potential to revive. As more people gain awareness and take small steps forward, things will improve. Education now helps students understand the implications of our acts on the ecology.

* There are certain organisations like PARI and Dastkar which bring awareness to these livelihoods. They showcase the work of artisans through exhibitions all over India.

CHAPTER NINE

Sustainable Development in the Leather Industry: A Study

OBJECTIVE

This essay aims to understand the different aspects of the leather industry, including its economic presence and environmental impact.

INTRODUCTION

For over 7,000 years, leather making has been practiced as an art. After hunting animals, people dried the animal skins in the sun. To soften the hides, skins were pounded in animal fats, and sometimes even animal brains or dung. They were preserved by salting and smoking the hides. Around 400 BC, the Egyptians and Hebrews developed the process of vegetable tanning that started off as simple drying and curing techniques. The Arabs preserved the art of leather making during the Middle Ages. This preservation led to improved leathers and added value to the Morocco and Cordovan leathers (from Spain). By the 15th century, leather tanning had become widespread. The Industrial Revolution and the introduction of power-driven machines assisted this growth. These machines were specialised to perform the tasks of splitting, fleshing, de-hairing, and so on. Chemical tannage was introduced towards the end of the 19th century.

PRODUCTION PROCESS

Cattle hide is the most often used (around 65%) in producing leather and its products. Sheep, goats and pigs account for another 34%. The remaining 1% comes from kangaroos, horses, and other less acceptable (endangered) animals. These include snakes and alligators.

1. PROCESS OF MAKING LEATHER (PRODUCTION PROCESS)

The leather-making process is an elaborate and time-consuming one. Additionally, manufacturing processes differ depending on the type of leather. To keep things simple, five key steps are common to different leathers. The process starts off with the preservation of raw hides until the finishing of the leather product.

Preservation:

This is also referred to as Pre-Tanning. After slaughtering, we obtain the raw materials (animal hide) needed to make leather. This needs to be stored carefully. Through preservation, temporary transport and storage of raw materials is made easy. This step is usually taken only if a tannery is not located nearby. Hides are first treated with salt to preserve them from bacterial action before being delivered to the tanneries.

Preparatory/ Beamhouse Operations:

The obtained hides are cleaned of all the dirt, blood, hair, and salt present. Since hides are fleshy in nature, extra bits are removed. After fleshing, the hides are coated with lime to chemically dissolve hair, remove unwanted proteins, and make the material flexible. Since the leather is still thick, the hide is divided into grain leather (from the top layer of the hide) and split leather (from the middle or low layer). Grain leather is made from the most external of the animal.

Tanning:

This is the process that transforms raw hides into what we call leather. Hides are placed inside a specially designed wooden rotating drum. Tanning agents like mineral salts and fish/animal oil convert raw fibres into durable leather. The pieces of leather are repeatedly wetted and dried. This aids in its preservation. After tanning, some steps like shaving (of excess parts), softening, and so on take place.

Post-tannage/Wet Finishing:

After hides go through the tannery to become leather, they undergo more steps. Syntan (Synthetic Tanning), fatliquors, and dyes are used on the leather to give it some final properties of texture and colour. Fatliquors are a type of emulsion, i.e., a mixture of liquids that normally do not mix, like oil and water.

Finishing:

This is the last part of the process of making leather. Leather is 'upgraded' by adding several layers of film. Some layers are designed to protect the leather, while other layers create fashionable patterns.

Finally, the finished leather pieces are sent to various factory outlets. From here, they are outsourced to local shops/branches.

PROCUREMENT RISKS

The value chain of leather includes many factors, such as labour costs, logistics, energy costs, etc. Suppliers are also operating with outdated technology, increasing the end cost significantly.

Since most countries import their leather, there are many risks in currency exchange. In some cases, buyer requirements are not clear. Cost buffers are built to face unprecedented risks. However, this increases the risk of overspending.

ECONOMIC PRESENCE

The Global Leather Goods Market size was valued at USD 419.5 billion in 2022. It is expected to expand at a CAGR (Compound Annual Growth Rate) of 6.2% from 2022 to 2030 and reach around USD 720.8 billion. With the highest revenue share, Europe has surpassed Asia as the leading region in the global leather goods market. But China remains the biggest exporter of finished leather products.

The leather industry plays an extremely important role in the Indian economy. Around 4.42 million people are employed in these industries.

Employment is especially prominent in rural areas of the country, with 30% of employees being women.

India is also a prominent player when it comes to the world economy. 13% of leather production (world) is accounted for by India. India is the second largest producer and consumer of leather footwear.

While Indian goats and sheep contribute to 11% of the world's total, buffalo and cattle populations contribute to 20%. Thus, India is a great source of raw material in the industry. It is important to note that the Government of India banned exports of raw material to protect the interests of manufacturing units within the country. However, India does export most of its finished leather goods. During 2021-22, India exported total leather and leather products of value US$ 4.87 billion, a 32% increase from the previous year. In August 2022, the total leather exports stood at US$ 473.87 million.

ENVIRONMENTAL IMPACT

Animals are killed for their meat every day. Since the skins of these animals are used for leather, the leather industry seems very sustainable at its essence. However, this is not the case when we look at the industry today. Although some leathers are marketed to be eco-friendly, the truth is far from it. The leather industry is, in fact, the most toxic industry due to the multiple ways in which it affects the environment.

A 2010 report published by the United Nations Industrial Development Organization summarised the different problems the leather industry was likely to face. Most of these are coming true in front of our eyes.

Air and Animals:

A major change has taken place in livestock production practices. Local multipurpose activity (between the meat and leather industries) has transformed into an intensive, market-oriented process (slaughtering animals).

'Slaughter animals' are raised for the very purpose of leather. This is a huge problem for the ecosystem. The raising of barn animals requires a lot of land for pasture and grazing as the animal grows up. Recently, studies have shown that over 70% of the Amazon rainforest has been cleared to create land for agricultural and grazing purposes.

Furthermore, barn animals, especially cows, are involved in the nitrogen cycle. This cycle leads to an increase in atmospheric nitrogen and other greenhouse gases. Cows release a lot of methane in their lifetime, contributing to this increase in atmospheric gas.

Normally, the natural methane in the air would be self-governed, but the scale is imbalanced with the growth of animals on such a large scale. This also means that the increasing proportion of livestock will lead to increased warmth and humidity, and thus, global warming.

Water:

Turning hide into leather, as we have seen, is not a simple process. It requires massive amounts of hazardous chemicals, including but not limited to mineral salts, chromium, and coal-tar derivatives. Some of the oils and dyes used are also cyanide-based, meaning they are poisonous once they find their way into waterways or groundwater. Although most production centres are based in the cities, the pollution, especially through water, can easily seep into the lives of people living hundreds of miles away.

Land:

Currently, there is a scramble for common property resources like grazing land and water. These are needed in abundance to bring up the slaughter animals, as well as to build tanneries and production centres. This means that there will be more large-scale industrial production that is located near urban centres. Owing to the dangerous nature of many of the processes and the chemicals used, this can be associated with environmental and public health risks, especially in the case of children and the elderly of the area.

Leather workers:

Many studies have proven the relationship between occupational cancers and people working at tanneries and leather factories.

Modern tanneries market the use of ear protectors, gloves, masks, and safety garments, along with careful monitoring of processes and proper cleaning. Despite these measures, many chemicals used to make leather are carcinogenic or likely to cause cancer. This increases the risk for leather workers to contract lung, pancreatic and bladder cancers. Exposure to leather dust can also lead to skin and nasal cancers.

REGULATIONS FOR SUSTAINABILITY

[Abbreviations used: CSIR - Council of Scientific and Industrial Research | CLRI - Central Leather Research Institute]

The leather industry in India is split into four sectors - Tanning, Footwear, Leather garments, and Leather garments and Accessories. Each of these sectors has its own regulations regarding sustainability.

In the Indian leather manufacturing avenue, CSIR-CLRI has introduced new technology in various forms. This includes the Waterless Chrome Tanning Process, introduced in 2015. Through this process, chrome tanning is carried out without water and avoids the use of acid, salts, and bases in the process. This ensures the saving of 15 million litres of water per day in the Indian sector alone.

CSIR-CLRI has implemented this process in multiple tanneries across India, as well as other countries such as Ethiopia, Sri Lanka, and Vietnam. In 2015, the then Indian Union minister (of science and technology), Dr. Harsh Vardhan, called the results a "paradigm shift."

Additionally, CLRI also succeeded in fostering an "enzymatic intervention." This means that fibre opening (during the production process)can be completed in a mere 30 minutes instead of 72 hours.

The Government of India has certain policies against animal cruelty. The Prevention of Cruelty to Animals Act (1960) is an example. Under a notification in 2017*, cattle (bulls, cows, buffaloes, oxen, calves and camels) can only be sold after a formal statement that they have not been brought to the market for sale for slaughter. The new rules of the Act aim at regulating the markets and sale of such animals.

VEGAN LEATHER AS AN ALTERNATIVE

Currently, many attempts are being made to produce ethically sourced leather. This is in support of protecting animal rights, as well as the conservation of the environment. Some people believe that leather should not be made with animals at all. They have thus come up with different ways of making leathers that are plant-based. These plant-based leathers are grouped together as vegan leather.

Plant-based leather includes those made from bamboo, banana, cacti, and mushrooms, along with different types of leaves (mulberry, teak). Leather is also made from polyurethane and called PU or faux (fake) leather.

Polyurethane is a plastic that has a similar texture to leather; in most cases, it is lighter in weight. However, it is not as durable as real leather and tends to tear easily. However, it is more resistant to sunlight, which is why it is commonly used to cover car seats and faux leather furniture. While real leather has genuine grain and slight imperfections in design, PU leather has an ideal patterned look. Also, PU leather is much easier to clean, and stains do not pose a big problem. PU leather is cheaper to produce and, thus, cheaper to purchase.

However, PU leather has its own set of repercussions. PU leather is known as the single most environmentally damaging type of plastic. It contains dioxins, which have been linked to cancer and developmental issues. They persist in the environment and are extremely harmful when burned.

---

* The notification was titled the Prevention of Cruelty to Animals (Regulation of Livestock Markets) Rules, 2017.

Therefore, which leather should be used is up to the consumer. If one feels deeply about animal cruelty, they can use vegan/PU leather products.

But if one feels deeply about the environment, it is better for them to use real leather products.

CHAPTER TEN

Urban Sprawl and Effective Planning: A Research Report

The four key concepts I explore in this essay:

- Urban sprawl
- Rehabilitation efforts
- Environmental inclusions in the cityscape; and
- how effective planning is integral to the outcome.

With regard to the aforementioned topics, I would like to specifically contrast the situations of the Tier 1 city of Chennai, Tamil Nadu, and the Tier 2 city of Chandigarh, Punjab, and Haryana [both Indian cities].

INTRODUCTION

Urbanisation refers to the process whereby a large number of people become concentrated in towns or cities, typical urban areas. Urbanisation naturally sets a precedent for a surge of commercial activity. Emigration for job-seeking, education, and the incentive of increased standard of living in tandem are some of the multiple contributory factors to the creation of urban centres.

As more people move to these areas in search of jobs, education, and an overall better standard of living, the city borders have to change. This change is to accommodate this ever-expanding population of present residents, the migrant working class and their relations, investors, and entrepreneurs, among other stakeholders.

Urbanisation is characterised by an increased expansion of man-made infrastructure compared to natural structures. When this expansion happens on a large scale due to changes in industry demands, such as the IT boom of Bangalore, it is called urban sprawl.

Urban or suburban sprawl refers to the phenomenon of unchecked expansion of cities and towns. This proliferation is facilitated by the need to accommodate an increasing population brought in by urbanisation of a particular area.

Initially, urban sprawl was considered a problem specific to the American subcontinent. As 'symptoms' of the phenomenon began to show up across the globe, it was recognised as a problem that needed rectification.

Expansion is also accompanied by a constant: **the peri-urban society**. These are generally referred to as the outskirts of the city, those on the periphery of being completely urban. A peri-urban area is typically classified by shifting economic activities from those of sustenance to those that are profit-oriented. Spatial changes are also most rapid in peri-urban areas. Since business centres are not too far away, and prices of land are much cheaper to set up commercial and residential establishments alike.

Chennai city in Tamil Nadu, India is a metropolitan- cosmopolitan city that is currently undergoing urban sprawl.

Urban sprawl was a term that I was familiar with, but the nature of the phenomenon was exposed to me through field trips to the areas of Semmencherry and Perumbakkam, on the outskirts of Chennai city.

METHODOLOGY

Field trips to the study areas involved secondary reading as prep. The NGO Thozhumai helped in interviewing various residents of the two areas. Thozhumai mainly focuses on the affairs of women and children in the areas. While their main office is in Adyar, they have ten activity centres spread across Semmenchery and Perumbakkam that teach adolescents life skills after school. The Perumbakkam office works with the police to raise awareness of child abuse, while the Semmencheri office ensures the education of the girl child and awareness of child marriage and child labour.

MAIN ESSAY

The idea behind choosing Chandigarh for my project was due to a one-day visit to the city of Chandigarh. It advertised itself as one of the most well-planned cities in the world, a notion that is strongly supported by residents and non-residents alike.

The fact that piqued my curiosity most was that a foreign architect had been invited to plan the city. Specifically, I wondered about the conception of city planning in an Indian setting, and its relevance in society.

Did it have as much effect as people made it out to be?

Chandigarh is acknowledged as being one of the world's well-planned cities. Chandigarh was chosen to be a planned city for various reasons. Politically, it was established as the state capital for both states of Punjab and Haryana in the year 1996. This, marked along with its recognition as a Union Territory, gave it significant importance. With reference to the environment, it was due to the availability of sufficient water supply, fertile soil, and gradient land, allowing for natural drainage, among others.

This essay has three parts:

- Corbusier's Plan for Chandigarh
- The trajectory of Chennai city, and
- Splitting of Zones - Patterns

Corbusier's Plan

The city was planned by the French architect Le Corbusier and his team consisting of Pierre Jeanrette, Maxwell Fry, and Jane Drew, along with a group of Indian architects - this list includes India's first female architect, Urmila Chowdury. Since Corbusier spearheaded it (he called himself its 'spiritual director'), the plan will hereafter be referred to as "Corbusier's plan" throughout the essay. Implementation of the plan was to take place in two phases - the first was under Corbusier and is the most well recognized.

Le Corbusier had designed multiple buildings around the world, but Chandigarh was to be his first major-scale project. The basis for the plan of Chandigarh city was to divide it into sectors that would house an approximate population of one million people. Demarcations further divide the sectors strategically into governmental, industrial, and residential areas. The sectors are further subdivided into urban villages and arranged concentrically; in Corbusier's words, 'a classified circulation pattern'.

Division of sectors

The term "urban village" refers to a phenomenon where villages are forcibly conjoined into cities to increase the territory of a city.

Urban villages are related to the concept of new urbanism, where areas within cities are categorised by walkability. Areas such as those used for parking lots are usually removed in favour of well-paved walkways. The idea behind the urban village is to make sure all amenities and essentials do not require an automobile to be reached.

Urban villages have the economic perks of urbanisation, such as inexpensive land rates; they suffer the degradation of the community sense that bound them together in the past. Urban villages come under the concept of new urbanism, a wing of sustainable planning. Theoretically, the implementation of different forms of new urbanism is supposed to lead to the absence of sprawling.

According to Corbusier's plan, each sector would have an average of 150 inhibitors, with each sector divided by a grid of traffic routes. By doing so, Corbusier aimed to avoid the major problems of other towns and cities - overcrowding, pavement dwelling, and setting up of shanties.

Under the National Policy of Rehabilitation/Resettlement and Land Acquisition, a Periphery Control Act was established. According to the Act, the controlled area was to be up to 10 miles on all sides of the boundary of the planned city. This was specifically for land acquired for the city before November 1st, 1966. No non-government-approved structure could be built in this extension of land. Only cattle sheds, mud/straw huts, and tube wells would be allowed within the defined border. This was aligned with the previously mentioned aim of Corbusier's plan.

The major role of aesthetics in the planning of Chandigarh is prominent in that each sector of the city is surrounded by flowering trees, shrubs, and other greenery. The sentiment of connectivity to nature was also found in the separate roads for cyclers and early-morning walkers; traffic junctions were centred around small circular parks, often having regional landmarks to please the eye of the common tourist. 'Green belts' were also included to ensure an inherent connection to nature. Currently, Chandigarh is home to the scenic Sukhna Lake, as well as the Rose and Rock Gardens, respectively.

Vertical and high-rise buildings were not included in the plan to take into account the socio-economic circumstances. It is inferred that this decision was meant to facilitate more interaction between people living in the same sector rather than a community setup within a gated area of apartments.

Corbusier introduced multiple buildings of aesthetic value, most notably the Capitol, an administrative compound of governmental activity. However, one area that failed to be covered in the first phase was that of rehabilitation. Many labourers originally from Chandigarh were called upon to transform these architectural beauties into actuality. They were not considered in the city plan at all, meaning that no specific houses or areas were designated for them to live in.

Constant construction activity over the years 1961-71 and 1981-91 also ensured the need for a larger workforce. Acknowledging this fact, more and more migrants moved to Chandigarh in the hopes of easy, steady employment. This triggered urban sprawl in the modernistic city.

Corbusier's aim of eradicating overcrowding and pavement dwelling went out in smoke as droves of workers struggled to find legal spaces to live in and carry out their life. This led to the existence of multiple slums surrounding the main city. A survey conducted in the 1970s states that there were approximately 4,500 slums in and around the city. This number rose to more than 8,000 by 1974.

The administration of Chandigarh city finally took up rehabilitation as an issue in 1975. The Licensing of Tenement and Transit Sites in Chandigarh Scheme was launched to rehabilitate slum dwellers in one-room tenements. As of 2008, 25% of Chandigarh's population lives in houses constructed by the Chandigarh Housing Board (CHB). While this resettlement/ rehabilitation scheme is considered to be effective, a survey performed in 2010 shows that an estimated 10% of Chandigarh's population live in unregistered slums.

Trajectory of Chennai city

Overlooking the Bay of Bengal, Chennai city is a vital vantage point through the lens of commercial activity.

Chennai was established as the state capital of Tamil Nadu upon India's independence in 1947, with its name legally changed in 1996. It has now grown to become one of India's many IT hubs. Chennai houses TIDEL Park, India's biggest IT park spanning nearly 12 acres. This cements the fact that Chennai is a bustling centre of South Indian trade.

The GCC or the Greater Chennai Corporation, established in 1688, is a municipal body tasked with the job of governing Chennai city - whose borders have recently been changed. Within the state of Tamil Nadu, the district of Chennai shares an invisible border with the districts of Kancheepuram, Chengalpet, and Tiruvallur. The borders of Chennai have been extended into the aforementioned districts to i) formally increase the Chennai Metropolitan Planning Area, thereby ii) increasing the jurisdiction of the GCC. This is according to the Notified Expansion Plan of 2022.

This change in borders has facilitated urban sprawl or rapid urban expansion of the city. One major contributory factor is that the Kancheepuram district is to get a new international airport. It is additionally claimed that the state government found it hard to cooperate with the lower forms of government over matters of relocation and slum dwellings and thus promoted this border regulation.

Semmenchery and Perumbakkam

Semmenchery and Perumbakkam, our interest areas, are two out of the 25 village panchayats that now come under the supervision of CMPA or Chennai Metropolitan Planning Area.

The 2004 tsunami affected more than 1800 families living in areas on and near the Marina beach - a vast majority were fisherfolk or involved in jobs relating to their immediate environment, the ocean. Since they lost their homes, the government gave them free housing in the newly established resettlement colony of Semmenchery. Housing in Semmenchery is characterised by blocks, or two-storey houses containing close to 10 houses, all 2 BHKs. A frequent question that is brought up is why people have been moved so far away from the place of their subsistence.

Barely a decade later, the 2015 floods massacred more houses and families. They were given housing in the Perumbakkam area. Perumbakkam's housing is slightly different. Rather than two-storeys, the Perumbakkam apartments are close to 12 storeys, with lifts, to accommodate more people.

Both areas have governmental facilities such as ration shops, primary and urban health centres. More recently, private schools and luxury high-rise apartments have come up around the resettlement areas. Apart from those affected by the flood, there have also been people who have moved to these areas for low-cost housing and land rates.

While these areas are situated in low-lying land, which is liable to frequent flooding, there are certain positives. With the establishment of the airport in Kancheepuram, the value of real estate increases while also increasing employment. This holds especially true for the hospitality and transport industries within the district. However, many have raised concerns about another relocation as the real estate value rises.

Urban sprawl in the industrial city of Chennai is a problem disguised as a solution. Urban sprawl is very closely related to the drainage of environmental resources, including increased rates of pollution, energy use, congestion, faulty infrastructure, and inadequate housing for all.

Splitting of zones - Patterns

Cities are categorised into tiers by the House Rent Allowance (HRA) Committee, which establishes rent rates depending on the degree to which a city is metropolitan. Cities are classified into X, Y and Z, more commonly referred to as Tier 1 and 2, and other cities. Chennai comes under Tier 1, while Chandigarh is under Tier 2. It is, therefore, unfair to compare the two in the traditional sense since governmental resource allocation is completely different for both cities.

Moreover, resource availability is also region-dependent, and both areas have different topographies - one is coastal, while the other is landlocked. However, for the purpose of understanding the differences and similarities between the cities, it would be interesting to see parallel patterns. I would like to briefly explore this specific to the splitting of a city into zones.

I mentioned that Chandigarh's plan revolved around walkability, the foundation of new urbanism. It is, therefore, interesting to note that due to the clear separation of zones, Corbusier and team actually made the city more dependent on vehicular transport. That is, people who resided within the city had to travel long distances to go to their place of work.

Despite the existence of multiple walkways and cycle paths, travelling from one sector to another via any mode of transport is still not time-efficient or economical - Since many in the working class could not afford private vehicles, they had to spend more money to travel to and from their workplace. This is similar to the situation in Semmenchery and Perumbakkam, where workers have either had to spend increasing amounts of income on travel or give up their traditional business entirely and pursue local, less rewarding jobs.

Thereby, the plan became an exact opposition to the very idea of new urbanism. Many modern planners thus advocate for mixed zoning as a learning from Chandigarh. Chennai is an example of [unplanned] mixed zoning.

Despite its present architectural planning backing, mixed zoning still poses a problem. Mainly, it is a subjective matter. There will always be those residents of a city that prefer privacy and security while others thrive for social connection. Mixed zoning also leads to lower quality of infrastructure and high rates of rent or ownership due to industrial proximity. This can lead to the establishment of more slum dwellings for cheaper land, as we have seen with Semmenchery and Perumbakkam.

Bibliography

Authoritarianism in Uganda under IDI AMIN

Kyemba, Henry. *A State of Blood : the Inside Story of Idi Amin.* New York: Grosset & Dunlap, 1977. Print.

Stevenson, William. *90 Minutes at Entebbe.* New York: Skyhorse Publishing, 1976. Print.

https://www.pewresearch.org/global/2019/03/25/a-sampling-of-public-opinion-in-india/

https://www.theguardian.com/news/2003/aug/18/guardianobituaries

https://www.britannica.com/biography/Idi-Amin

https://www.pbs.org/tpt/dictators-playbook/episodes/idi-amin/

https://artsandculture.google.com/story/idi-amin-dada-never-a-dull-moment-mohamed-amin-foundation/CwVhlWoDA5nrKA?hl=en

https://adst.org/2016/08/rise-power-butcher-uganda/

https://www.amnesty.org/en/wp-content/uploads/2021/06/afr590071978en.pdf

https://www.nytimes.com/1972/09/13/archives/amin-praises-hitler-for-killing-of-jews.html

https://www.repository.cam.ac.uk/bitstream/handle/1810/284104/George%20Roberts%20JEAS%20revised%20text.docx?sequence=1&isAllowed=y

NOTIONS OF GENDER IN POPULAR MEDIA

Video components:

[1] https://www.youtube.com/watch?v=RId_UXL3rI8&themeRefresh=1

Seagram Imperial Blue's "Men will be men" ad campaign: Anniversary edition, 2011

[2] https://www.youtube.com/watch?v=hNqwBTCslMw

Titan Raga's "#BreakTheBias", 2016

[3] https://www.youtube.com/watch?v=UYaY2Kb_PKI

Gillette's "The Best Men Can Be", 2019 [from The Guardian's channel]

[4] https://www.merriam-webster.com/dictionary/gender

[5] https://books.google.com/ngrams/graph?content=gender&year_s

tart=1800&year_end=2019&corpus=en-2019&smoothing=7

Google Books NGram Viewer, Use of the word 'gender' from 1800 - 2019

[6] https://en.oxforddictionaries.com/definition/stereotype

[7] https://www.asa.org.uk/static/uploaded/e06425f9-2f9f-44c3-ae6ebd 5902686d44.pdf

Depictions, Perceptions and Harm: A Report on Gender Stereotypes in Advertising - ASA (Advertising Standards Authority) of the UK.

[8]https://www.businessinsider.in/advertising/brands/article/have-women-had-enough-of-imperial-blues-men-will-be-men-ads-women-from-the-ad-and-marketing-world-tell-us-their-thoughts/articleshow/78644475.cms

Have women had enough of Imperial Blue's "Men Will Be Men" Ads?

Thoughts from women in the Advertising and Marketing world.

[9]https://www.youtube.com/watch?v=c57Km2hOKrI

Controversial Gillette ad asks "Is this the best a man can get?" - CBS News

A short coverage of the ad on American broadcast/ television

[10] https://www.forbes.com/sites/avidan/2019/01/16/for-men-gillette-is-no-longer-the-best-a-brand-can-get/?sh=4044efa5ea57

For men, Gillette is no longer the best a man can get - Forbes

An article taking a negative stance on the Gillette ad campaign

[11]https://www.forbes.com/sites/michelleking/2019/01/20/gillette-responds-to-controversial-advert-challenging-toxic-masculinity/?sh=79af584b5bb7

Gillette responds to controversial advert challenging toxic masculinity

An interview with the VP of Global Communications at P&G

PARENTAL RELATIONSHIPS AND SPECIAL EDUCATION for PwDs

Haddon, Mark. The Curious Incident of the Dog in the Night-time. Oxford: David Fickling Books, 2003

Rao, Shankar C. "Role and Status", "Power - Authority - Status", "Marriage", "The Family" *Sociology.* S. Chand, 2019

Disability rights: Education - GOV.UK (https://www.gov.uk/rights-disabled-person/education-rights)

Children with special educational needs and disabilities (SEND): Overview - GOV.UK

(https://www.gov.uk/children-with-special-educational-needs)

NHS England » Special educational needs and disability (SEND)

Learning and your rights | nidirect

(https://www.nidirect.gov.uk/articles/learning-and-your-rights

Timeline - How Was School?

(https://howwasschool.allfie.org.uk/timeline/)

Education of Individuals with Autism - History, Schools' Responses and Methods of Teaching, Goals and Purposes of Education - StateUniversity.com

(https://education.stateuniversity.com/pages/1779/Autism-Education-Individuals-with.html)

What's Going On? The Question of Time Trends in Autism

(https://www.ncbi.nlm.nih.gov/pmc/articles/PMC1497666/pdf/15504445.pdf)

ECNI - Schools, Education Service Providers, Equality Commission, Northern Ireland

(https://www.equalityni.org/Schools)

Language Log: A brief history of "spaz"

Spaz Definition & Meaning - Merriam-Webster

Why Do People Have Repressed Anger? | Psychology Today

RURAL LIVELIHOODS: IS THERE A FUTURE?

[1] https://www.merriam-webster.com/dictionary/livelihood

[2] https://ich.unesco.org/en/traditional-craftsmanship-00057

[3] https://scialert.net/fulltext/?doi=rjf.2016.1.7

[4] https://www.india.gov.in/topics/art-culture/handicrafts

[5] https://www.greavesindia.co.uk/the-tamil-nadu-handicrafts-to-bring-home/

[6] https://www.craftscouncilofindia.in/indian-crafts-map/tamil-nadu/

[7] https://www.mapsofindia.com/maps/crafts/

[8] https://india.mongabay.com/2019/02/why-tamil-nadu-needs-more-palmyrah-the-state-tree/

[9] https://www.downtoearth.org.in/blog/wildlife-biodiversity/why-india-must-conserve-its-palm-trees-73343

[10] https://timesofindia.indiatimes.com/city/gurgaon/fading-demand-for-diyas-spells-darkness-for-potters-this-diwali/articleshow/66503415.cms

[11] https://pib.gov.in/PressReleasePage.aspx?PRID=1606279

[12] Karthikeyan, Aparna. "Fifty Feet Above..." *Nine Rupees an Hour.* Context (imprint of Westland Publications Private Limited), 2019. Print.

[13] https://ncert.nic.in/textbook/pdf/jess203.pdf

SUSTAINABLE DEVELOPMENT IN THE LEATHER INDUSTRY: A STUDY

https://www.ibef.org/exports/leather-industry-india

Leather Industry - an overview | ScienceDirect Topics

Toxic Waste From Leather Industries - ScienceDirect

https://www.peta.org/issues/animals-used-for-clothing/leather-industry/leather-environmental-hazards/

https://www.researchgate.net/publication/310457762_THE_IMPACT_OF_THE_LEATHER_INDUSTRY_LEFT_ON_THE_ENVIRONMENT

http://www.madehow.com/Volume-2/Leather-Jacket.html

The social impact of leather | Somewhat Greener

Your Guide to Vegan Leather (February 2020) | PETA

https://www.ncbi.nlm.nih.gov/pmc/articles/PMC3168109/ (Occupational cancers in leather tanning industries)

https://undark.org/2017/02/21/leather-tanning-bangladesh-india/

https://www.harpersbazaar.com/uk/fashion/fashion-news/a30640996/vegan-leather-sustainability/

https://www.popsci.com/environment/leather-sustainability-ethics/

https://ethicalmadeeasy.com/is-vegan-leather-actually-better-for-the-environment/

https://www.unep.org/news-and-stories/story/methane-emissions-are-driving-climate-change-heres-how-reduce-them

https://leatherpanel.org/sites/default/files/publications-attachments/future_trends_in_the_world_leather_and_leather_products_industry_and_trade.pdf

https://www.ibef.org/exports/leather-industry-india

https://www.solidaridadnetwork.org/story/india-steps-up-to-make-leather-production-more-sustainable/

https://www.sciencedirect.com/science/article/pii/S2666821121000247

https://www.clri.org/CLRIMagazine/LEATHERPostApril2018.pdf

https://www.clri.org/docs/2021/2Clri-E-Brocher-2021.pdf

https://textilevaluechain.in/news-insights/process-of-leather-making/

https://www.leather-dictionary.com/index.php/Leather_production

https://www.neratanning.com/knowledge/the-leather-making-process-step-by-step/

https://www.linkedin.com/pulse/rising-demand-leather-products-government-support-industry-thomus

https://www.globenewswire.com/en/news-release/2022/08/22/2502449/0/en/Leather-Goods-Market-Size-is-projected-to-reach-USD-720-8-Billion-by-2030-growing-at-a-CAGR-of-6-2-Straits-Research.html

https://leatherpanel.org/sites/default/files/publications-attachments/future_trends_in_the_world_leather_and_leather_products_industry_and_trade.pdf

https://hub.unido.org/sites/default/files/publications/Occupational%20safety%20and%20health%20aspects%20of%20leather%20manufacturing_2021.pdf

https://www.satra.com/bulletin/article.php?id=2576

https://www.worstpolluted.org/projects_reports/display/88

https://www.researchgate.net/publication/337724099_Water_Pollution_Caused_by_Leather_Industry_A_Review

https://www.nomomente.org/post/faux-leather-vs-real-leather

URBAN SPRAWL

https://www.architectural-review.com/buildings/chandigarh-once-the-future-city

https://urbanplanning.chd.gov.in/assets/pdf/1591863879-PlanningArchitecture_pdf.pdf

https://chandigarh.gov.in/sites/default/files/documents/commercial.pdf

Commercial centres of Chandigarh

https://chandigarh.gov.in/know-chandigarh/planning-architecture/after-le-corbusier

Chandigarh after Le Corbusier

https://scroll.in/magazine/1019474/what-le-corbusier-got-wrong-and-right-in-his-design-of-chandigarh

https://www.researchgate.net/profile/Ramakrishna-Nallathiga/publication/336891271_Housing_for_the_Urban_Poor_The_Case_of_Chandigarh_Model/links/5db94f05458515l435dlb42b/Housing-for-the-Urban-Poor-The-Case-of-Chandigarh-Model.pdf

Housing for Urban Poor in Chandigarh - An Essay

https://upload.indiacode.nic.in/showfile?actid=AC_CH_60_901_00001_00001_1548411178914&type=regulation&filename=implementation_of_national_rehablitation_and_resettlement_scheme,2009.pdf

Chandigarh Government, 'Implementation of National Rehabilitation and Resettlement Scheme, 2009', Chandigarh Administration Gazette (Extra)

https://www.linkedin.com/advice/3/what-some-benefits-challenges-mixed-use-development#:~:text=However%2C%20mixed%2Duse%20development%20also,and%20affordability%20of%20[th]e%20spaces.

https://www.downtoearth.org.in/coverage/urban-villages--an-oxymoron-13014

https://www.freethink.com/culture/urban-villages

http://admser.chd.nic.in/uploadfiles/press/advt/NATIONAL%20POLICY%20OF%20REHABILITATION11111.pdf - Resettlement/Rehabilitation policies

https://chennaimetrorail.org/wp-content/uploads/2019/03/Chennai-Metro-Phase-2map.pdf

https://chennai.nic.in/history/

https://chennaicorporation.gov.in/gcc/about-GCC/greater-chennai-corporation/brief-note-about-GCC/

https://www.cmdachennai.gov.in/CMPA-Expansion.html

Other Books
by Shraddha Anu Shekar

Mahishasura Marketer: Lessons from Mythology to slay marketing Demons! (2022)

The Ghatotkacha Game: Marketing lessons from Mythology (2020)

Shalya: Stories from the Mahabharatha (2020)

Muruga – The God of War (2018)

The Adventures of Morty: The famous Turtle Detective (2016)

All books available at: https://t.ly/s0OV8

www.ingramcontent.com/pod-product-compliance
Lightning Source LLC
LaVergne TN
LVHW091036150826
845672LV00006BA/1843

* 9 7 9 8 8 9 2 3 3 5 8 5 0 *